# HEARST CASTLE

## The Story of William Randolph Hearst and San Simeon

by
Taylor Coffman

A SEQUOIA BOOK

ACADEMY OF MOTION PICTURE ARTS AND SCIENCES: P. 50 top, 64 right. ROBERT ADKISSON: P. 35 top right, 57 top, 65 top, 88 top right, 90 top. THE BANCROFT LIBRARY, UNIVERSITY OF CALIFORNIA, BERKELEY: P. 13, 20, 21 bottom, 24, 25. CALIFORNIA PRESS ASSOCIATION (JOHN HEALEY COLLECTION): P. 27. TAYLOR COFFMAN: P. 23, 89, 93. PETER D'APRIX (COURTESY OF CALIFORNIA STATE PARKS FOUNDATION: P. 44-45, 47 right, 66 top left, 67, 79 bottom, 80 bottom left, 81 top, 82, 83 top right, 84 top. MARK DOLYAK: Inside back cover top. BURTON FREDERICKSEN: P. 43, 47 left, 83 top left, 86. PAT HATHAWAY COLLECTION: P. 15 top, 22 bottom. HEARST SAN SIMEON STATE HISTORICAL MONUMENT, SAN SIMEON REGION, STATE OF CALIFORNIA DEPARTMENT OF PARKS AND RECREATION: P. 9, 32 bottom, 38 right, 50 bottom, 56 bottom, 58 bottom, 66 right. DR. ROBERT HOOVER (EDITH WEBB COLLECTION): P. 16 bottom. ROBERT LATSON: P. 2-3, back cover, front & back flap, 10-11, 15 bottom, 21 top, 26 top, 28, 34, 39 top, 41 top left, 42 left, 46 right, 59 right, 61 top, 74 bottom, 85 top, 88 bottom, 90 bottom left & right, 91 bottom, inside back cover bottom. GEORGE LEPP: Inside front cover & p. 1. PABLO MASON: P. 35 bottom. OLD MISSION SAN ANTONIO ARCHIVES: P. 17. OLD MISSION SANTA BARBARA ARCHIVES: P. 16 top. PRINCETON UNIVERSITY LIBRARY: P. 14. PRIVATE SOURCES: P. 27 bottom, 29, 51, 64 left, 65 bottom left, 88 left, inside back cover middle. MARJORIE RAMSAY: P. 42 bottom. KEN RAVEILL: P. 5, 48-49, 52 top, 53, 54-55, 68 top, 72, 73, 74 top, 75, 76-77, 78 top, 79 top right, 80 top & bottom right, 81 bottom, 83 bottom, 85 bottom, 87, 91 top, 94-95. J. C. SEBASTIAN: P. 32 top. KIRBY SHAW & XANDRA FISHER-SHAW, OCEANA MAPS: P. 96. SEA LANDING, INC.: P. 22 top. MABEL SOUZA: P. 52 bottom. SPECIAL COLLECTIONS, CALIFORNIA POLYTECHNIC STATE UNIVERSITY, SAN LUIS OBISPO: P. 18, 19, 26 bottom, 30, 33, 36 bottom, 37, 38 left & bottom, 39 bottom, 40, 41 bottom, 42 top, 46 left, 57 bottom, 58 top & bottom left top, 59 left, 61 bottom, 65 bottom right, 66 bottom left, 68 bottom. JOHN WHITE: P. 6-7, 62-63, 78 bottom, 79 top left. CARLETON M. WINSLOW, JR.: Cover, 8-9, 56 top, 60, 70-71, 92. MYRON WILCOX ESTATE: P. 39 top left. BARON WOLMAN: P. 12, 69.

# PREFACE

*Portrait of William Randolph Hearst by Orrin Peck, 1894*

The story of Hearst Castle has been told many times before and undoubtedly will be told many times again. Is there such a thing, though, as *the* story of Hearst Castle? Not exactly, at least not yet—not while extensive research remains to be done. Diversity, complexity, vastness, and no small measure of enticing mystery characterize "Hearstiana," making the historian's task formidable but always rewarding.

I began to probe the history surrounding the Castle shortly after I started working at Hearst Monument in 1972. Irene Horne, Supervisor of Guides, encouraged my research from the very outset; I owe her many thanks for her support.

In 1980, Donald Ackland of Sequoia Communications, gave me my first chance to break into print. We have looked forward to working together on this new book ever since.

John Porter, my editor and very close friend, deserves my utmost praise and gratitude for his literary expertise and thoughtful copyediting.

John also typed a letter-perfect final draft of the manuscript.

I am grateful to Nancy Loe, Head of Special Collections at California Polytechnic State University, for allowing me to include several excerpts from the correspondence in the Julia Morgan Collection, most of which have never been published until now.

Sara Holmes Boutelle and Maurice Hudkins deserve my thanks, as do Carol Everingham, whose "Dateline" of the Hearst-Morgan correspondence proved very useful, and Robert Latson, who guided me through the Hearst Castle architectural drawings. Victoria Kastner carefully transcribed for me some of the Arthur Byne correspondence in the Julia Morgan Collection; she and her husband, George, also read parts of the text and made many helpful suggestions.

In addition, Ronald Whaley, Brother Timothy Arthur, and Susan Roberts-Manganelli read parts of the text and offered constructive criticism, as did James Anders of ARA Leisure

Services, Inc. So did Mrs. William Randolph Hearst, Jr., who also shared with me some of her extensive knowledge of the Hearst family.

I also wish to thank Kirby Shaw and Xandra Fisher-Shaw for the lovely map they produced for the book. Dr. Robert Hoover and especially Robert Gibson provided authoritative information on the Chumash Indians. Both Byron Hanchett and Frances Souza Scott shared illuminating reminiscences with me. The Hearst San Simeon State Historical Monument staff deserves my gratitude as well, particularly Deborah Weldon, Gerry Norgaard, Norman Rotanzi, Metta Hake, Jeffry Payne, Carolyn Martin, Sandra Buchman, Sally Scott, and Julie Payne.

Finally, I extend the most heartfelt thanks to my wife and daughters for sharing my love and enthusiasm for the Castle and for standing by patiently while I experienced the usual travails of authorship.

*The Three Graces*

# CONTENTS

*William Randolph Hearst's private Gothic Study on the third floor of Casa Grande epitomizes the diversity and grandeur of La Cuesta Encantada.*

*Point Piedras Blancas, whose lighthouse was built in 1874, boldly punctuates the California coastline near Hearst Castle.*

# Part 1

# PRELUDE TO GRANDEUR

**H**earst Castle and San Simeon, San Simeon and Hearst Castle —because we often interchange the two names, they seem one and the same. Almost everyone knows what "Hearst Castle" means. We recognize the name far and wide as a catchword for the palatial estate built by William Randolph Hearst on a faraway, scenic California hilltop—an architectural wonder whose real name is *La Cuesta Encantada* or, when translated from the Spanish, "The Enchanted Hill." But *San Simeon*, another Spanish name, is something else again; though we mention it nearly as often as "Hearst Castle," its meaning can be a bit elusive. "Where exactly is San Simeon?" visitors to the Castle often ask. "Who chose that name? What does *San Simeon* mean?"

Far more than a synonym for Hearst Castle, *San Simeon* applies to a picturesque seaside village, to a creek and its backcountry reaches, to an old Mexican land grant, to an abrupt, jagged point of land that is actually an earthquake fault jutting into the Pacific—in other words, to an area, a micro-region, a little corner of California. From the open grazing land near the lower end of the Hearst Ranch, east along the creek that bears Saint Simeon's name and up to the

Santa Lucia crest; north along the summit, past Rocky Butte and Pine Mountain; west, curving along the hills behind the Castle and continuing past the peaks that mark the beginning of the Big Sur country, and back to the shoreline at San Carpoforo Creek—this crescent of mountain and foothill, coastal plain and shoreline is San Simeon. Isolated from the rest of the world except where it gives way to the forested hills of Cambria, San Simeon long remained a land apart, a California principality guarded by the Coast Range on one side and the Pacific Ocean on the other. At a point almost exactly in the center of San Simeon lies the island ridge capped by Hearst Castle, an architectural jewel in a pristine, near-wilderness setting. A finer orchestration of elements can scarcely be imagined.

San Simeon's early heritage is Spanish and Mexican, which is reflected in place names typical of that part of California where the Hispanic culture took hold. However prosaic many of these names sound when translated, they evoke an unsurpassed sense of history. Some of them are merely descriptive. Rivulets and gulches, for example, that crossed the rough coastal trail were typically called *arroyos*: Arroyo Laguna, Arroyo de los Chinos, Arroyo de la Cruz, and, marking the boundary between the Piedra Blanca and the San Simeon grants, Arroyo del Padre Juan. Others are commemorative of saints. Sebastian Vizcaino, the Spanish explorer, gave this segment of the Coast Range the name *Santa Lucia* when he sailed past in 1602. Ironically, the origin of *San Simeon*, the one name that speaks for an entire locality— which includes the world-renowned Castle—has yet to be definitively traced. The existing evidence indicates that the name was bestowed by the padres at San Miguel, the Franciscan mission situated some twenty-five miles inland along El Camino Real.

Mission San Miguel was founded in 1797. By 1810 it had extended its sphere of activity westward over the Santa Lucias and down to the water's edge. A short distance upstream from the mouth of San Simeon Creek, very close to what is now a state beach campground, San Miguel established

a village outpost near the site of a former Indian settlement known in the extinct Chumash tongue as Stajahuayo. Perhaps Saint Simeon's unusual character had some special significance for the *rancheria*, as such establishments were called. The *Book of Saints* relates that Saint Simeon Stylites, who lived in fifth-century Syria, "adopted his characteristic fashion of sanctifying his soul by doing penance and praying on top of a lofty stone column. In it he persevered for 37 years. From time to time he increased the height of his pillar." Because of the restricted space on top of the column, Saint Simeon "could stand, kneel or sit, but never lie down. . . . His whole life was in a sense a miracle." But whatever inspired this saint's commemoration is unknown; at any rate, the first recorded mention of San Simeon as this remote coastal satellite dates from 1819.

In 1827 Juan Cabot, a priest at San Miguel, reported to the Mexican

governor on the status of the Mission's holdings, giving a glimpse of the prosperous though hard life enjoyed by the California missions before their rapid decline at the hands of secularization:

> *From the Mission to the beach the land consists almost entirely of mountain ridges, devoid of permanent water. For this reason that region is not occupied until one reaches the coast where the Mission has a house of adobe. Here it may cultivate some clear land for planting grain in summer time but it is entirely dependent upon rain, since there is no irrigated land there. In the same district 800 cattle, some tame horses and breeding mares are kept at said* Rancho, *which is called* San Simeon.

*San Simeon village and its curving white-sand beach nestle in the lee of rugged San Simeon Point. Highway 1 and the Hearst Monument Visitor Center can be seen in the background.*

Though only the most limited traces of the old settlement remain, the sketchy details surrounding this far-removed frontier outpost provide a view of the early Hispanic background of the district. They also provide a glimpse of San Simeon's earliest heritage, which, in a manner sadly typical of most California Indian cultures, was rapidly subjugated to the point of extinction.

In their zealous attempt to Christianize the native populations, the Spaniards gathered up the Indians for relocation at the mission compounds. Virtually all human inhabitants were eventually removed from certain localities, among them the San Simeon area, from which the Indians were sent to San Miguel and the neighboring missions of San Antonio and San Luis Obispo. At the missions, the Indians, mingling with those from elsewhere, gradually lost their tribal and linguistic distinctions. Researchers have only now begun to identify correctly the original inhabitants of the San Simeon area. Traditionally the Indians of this district have been regarded as coastal representatives of the Salinan culture. The Spanish word *Playano*, or beach people, has also cropped up, but how exactly it should be applied has been disputed. The current theory designates San Simeon as the northernmost extension of the Chumash, the Indians who held the coast from Malibu and Santa Barbara northward but who were formerly thought to have given way to the Salinans in the vicinity of Morro Bay. Now the Chumash are believed to have spread farther up the coast to the point where they encountered the great barrier of San Carpoforo. Additional studies must be made before boundary lines can be conclusively drawn, but scholars have already resurrected some of the original Indian place names of the region: exotic, often lyrical names like Tissimassu, Zay, Tsetacol, and Zaha Saltanel, names that passed into oblivion after the coming of the Spaniards.

*Known as the "Mission on the Highway," San Miguel Arcangel is situated ten miles north of Paso Robles along modern-day U.S. Highway 101, formerly El Camino Real. Although founded nearly thirty years later than the neighboring missions of San Antonio and San Luis Obispo, San Miguel is the one that left an enduring name on the coastal area near Hearst Castle—San Simeon.*

Juan Rodriguez Cabrillo, who discovered California while searching for the fabled Northwest Passage, sailed by the San Simeon coast late in 1542 but, contrary to an old story that he anchored in San Simeon Bay, made no landfall anywhere in the area. From offshore Cabrillo reported "no population or smokes," and he observed that "all the coast, which has no shelter on the north, is uninhabited." Sixty years later Sebastian Vizcaino sailed northward toward his discovery of Monterey Bay, named the Santa Lucia Range enroute, and made only limited reference to native inhabitants. It remained for a land party—the Sacred Expedition of 1769 led by Gaspar de Portola—to make the first known European contact with the Indians of the region. The diarists in the group, Father Juan Crespi most notably, tell a tale far different from that told by the early mariners.

Entering the greater area toward mid-September, the members of the Sacred Exhibition encountered some sixty Indians near what is now Cambria, continued into the San Simeon area and the present-day Hearst Ranch, and camped at what would later be named Pico Creek in honor of Jose de Jesus Pico. The next day they proceeded into the heart of the region, noting San Simeon Point on their left. They veered inland along an Indian trail, approximately where the Hearst Ranch airstrip is today, crossed the low divide into lovely Arroyo de la Cruz, camped near a large pool that would one day be a swimming hole for the Hearsts, and encountered six Indians.

Wednesday, September 13, found the members of the Expedition at the foot of the Big Sur country, where the cliffs beyond San Carpoforo Creek stopped their passage up the coast and forced them to turn inland. (The Big Sur stopped not only Portola in 1769 but nearly everyone else until Highway I was blasted through after World War I.)

The next few days were as arduous as anything Portola had experienced; the path would undoubtedly have been harder still if the local Indians had not established a trail over the Santa Lucias years earlier. Finally,

*Juan Rodriguez Cabrillo, the first European to sail past San Simeon. Other mariners followed in Cabrillo's wake, but none went ashore any closer than Morro Bay. The Sacred Expedition of 1769, a land party led by Gaspar de Portola in search of Monterey, was the first to set foot in the San Simeon area.*

though, the Expedition penetrated the backcountry maze and reached the Nacimiento River palisades—a scenic narrows through which W. R. Hearst and his guests would one day ride—and the oak-studded country that would soon be the setting for Mission San Antonio de Padua.

Three months later Portola, on his return trek, saw more Indians than he had seen on the way up. Colder inland temperatures coupled with ideal shellfishing conditions during the winter months may have prompted an influx to the coastal edge. Evidently the season was also religiously significant. At their Christmas Eve encampment near Cambria, Portola's party saw as many as 250 Indians participating in a solstice celebration that had attracted people from miles around.

These original inhabitants were superbly adapted to their coastal environment; yet within a single

generation of Portola, Spanish colonization would spell their doom. Today their ghosts remain in the artifacts that farmers and ranchers have unearthed while working their fields.

In 1770 Portola passed through San Simeon on a second trip, observed a group of forty Indians at Stajahuayo (San Simeon Creek), struggled over the San Carpoforo trail once more, and finally succeeded in recognizing Monterey Bay as the spot that Vizcaino had glowingly described nearly two hundred years earlier. A mission and a presidio were established at Monterey, and in 1771 Junipero Serra, the father of the California missions, followed up Portola's groundwork by founding the third mission in the chain, San Antonio de Padua, in a remote valley twenty-five miles north of Hearst Castle.

*Left: The construction of Highway 1 along the Big Sur coast included some spectacular bridge-building, most notably at Bixby Creek near Carmel.*

*Below: The coastal plain north of Point Piedras Blancas ends abruptly at San Carpoforo Creek, beyond which the Santa Lucia Range rises steeply from the Pacific for the next seventy-five miles. Not until 1937 was the precarious toehold of Highway 1 finally established along this mountain barrier.*

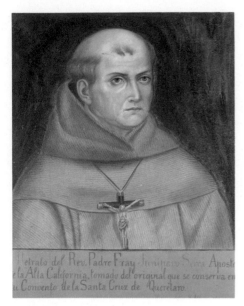

*Junipero Serra (1713–84), Franciscan padre and founder of the first nine of the twenty-one California missions. Serra's third mission, San Antonio de Padua, was established in 1771 in an isolated valley that later became part of the Hearst Ranch.*

*Mission San Antonio de Padua as it appeared about a century after its founding.*

San Antonio was destined to play a role in the early history of San Simeon equal to that played by San Miguel, especially since Rancho Piedra Blanca fell within its territory. In later years the historical currents would flow the other way, with the Hearsts playing a significant role in San Antonio's history. About 1900 Phoebe Apperson Hearst would sponsor archaeological work near the mission, and shortly before World War I her son, W. R. Hearst, would begin increasing the family's ranch holdings in the area. After Phoebe Hearst's death, her son would embark on an even greater expansion of his parents' original property, buying the bulk of five Mexican land grants, aggregating more than 100,000 acres. Half a mile from the mission compound he would build the sprawling Milpitas Hacienda at Jolon as a modern compliment to the mission, and in 1948 he would establish a fund of half a million dollars for the restoration of the California missions, $50,000 of which would go to San Antonio.

*Late 1880s photograph of the Encinales Indian family, taken at Mission San Antonio. The matriarch, Perfecta Encinales (fourth from left), was a neophyte at San Antonio in the days before secularization and was a renowned basket-maker.*

The spheres of interest of both Mission San Antonio and Mission San Miguel overlapped in the San Simeon area. Both had their eyes on San Simeon Bay, which by the beginning of the nineteenth century had become an occasional port of call for whalers, fur-trading vessels, and hide-and-tallow ships from New England. Foreign commerce was technically forbidden under Spanish rule, but because supplies were slow to reach Upper California from far-away Mexico, the missions partook of trading opportunities when they could. Beyond providing mere necessities, the traffic in horses, sea otter pelts, cattle hides, and other commodities was potentially lucrative. But no sooner had the missions become prosperous than newly independent Mexico made the mission lands available for private use and ownership. Stripped of their power and prestige through the process known as secularization, the missions fell quickly into ruin.

Meanwhile the splendors of California were becoming known to the outside world through the writings of seamen and adventurers who had seen the coast from offshore or who had actually visited the missions. Richard Henry Dana's book *Two Years Before the Mast* is the premier account of California in those pastoral years. Dana, who was on the coast in 1835, does not refer to San Simeon; however, in *Life in California*, Alfred Robinson, who visited San Miguel about 1830, gives what is probably the earliest description of San Simeon except for the accounts in the mission annals:

> At the distance of about 5 leagues is a beautiful little bay called St. Simeon. Its anchorage is safe, and well protected from the winds, yet it is seldom visited by navigators.

Another contemporary account is that of the French diplomat Eugene Duflot de Mofras, who was in California in 1841 and who visited the San Simeon area by way of Mission San Antonio:

> Sheltered by a slight eminence, 8 leagues above Los Esteros and 7 from San Miguel Mission, lies the mooring place known as San Simeon. This is open to the northwesterly trade winds, and has 5 or 6 fathoms of water close to shore. Not far from the beach stands a rancho. From here on up as far north as Monterey the coast is marked by several promontories or small capes at the foot of the Santa Lucia Mountains that assume protection from the prevailing summer breezes. This anchorage should prove quite valuable at some future date when the thick woods that dot the mountains acquire commercial value.

A cartographer as well, Duflot de Mofras published a map of the California coast in 1844. His inclusion of San Simeon Bay marked the first charting of this locally important landform. Duflot de Mofras also noted that the little harbor was regularly used as an anchorage, an observation suggesting that trade had increased since the time of Robinson's visit.

*A fund of $500,000 provided by the Hearst Foundation in 1948 helped restore San Antonio and other California missions to their former glory.*

S an Simeon Bay continued to be at least a sporadic port of call until the time of California statehood in 1850, when steadier use accompanied the influx of American settlers to the greater area. The choicest sections of San Simeon were held by a small number of landowners, chief among them Jose de Jesus Pico. In 1840 Pico had been granted the Rancho de la Piedra Blanca—the Ranch of the White Rock—or simply Piedra Blanca, which included the fifteen miles of coastal plain Mission San Antonio had used as summer pasturage. Piedra Blanca comprised 48,805 acres —nearly the maximum allowable size for a Mexican grant—and extended from Arroyo del Padre Juan at its lower end, past San Simeon Bay and the huge white rocks that gave rise to the plural form "Piedras Blancas," and

on to the steep canyon at San Carpoforo. Inland the grant encompassed the ridge that became La Cuesta Encantada and continued up the main slopes of the Santa Lucias to a line just below the summit. The present-day Hearst Ranch includes nearly all of Piedra Blanca as it stood in the mid-nineteenth century.

The adjoining Rancho San Simeon grant was only a tenth as large, taking up the coastal wedge between Piedra Blanca and San Simeon Creek. Another prominent *Californio,* Jose Ramon Estrada, was granted Rancho San Simeon in the early 1840s, but he sold the entire parcel three years later; thereafter, a series of other sales and subdivisions followed, too complex to

*One of architect Julia Morgan's least known but most impressive structures, the Milpitas Hacienda served through the 1930s as headquarters for William Randolph Hearst's ranch operations in the area surrounding Mission San Antonio.*

*Hearst made Milpitas a rustic equivalent of San Simeon by using Navajo blankets and other provincial furnishings. The building was sold to the United States Government in 1940, along with more than 150,000 acres of adjoining Hearst ranch land, and is now part of Fort Hunter Liggett.*

disentangle. Part of Rancho San Simeon eventually came under Hearst ownership, forming a southeastern corner for the great ranch that is otherwise dominated by Piedra Blanca and usually identified with it.

But for all their wealth in land, the *Californios* were ill-equipped to survive the turbulent 1850s and '60s. The Act of 1851 put the burden of proof upon them as they sought to have their land titles confirmed by the United States Government. Litigation could drag on for years, leaving many a landowner the victim of legal fees and usurious interest rates before his grant was patented. Even worse for the old aristocracy was the great drought of 1863-64, which decimated livestock and left the land parched and sterile. Jose de Jesus Pico was ruined, and Piedra Blanca would change hands completely during the next fifteen years, mostly through a series of sales to George Hearst, a rich mining baron and the father of a more famous Hearst, the Hearst who half a century later would create La Cuesta Encantada.

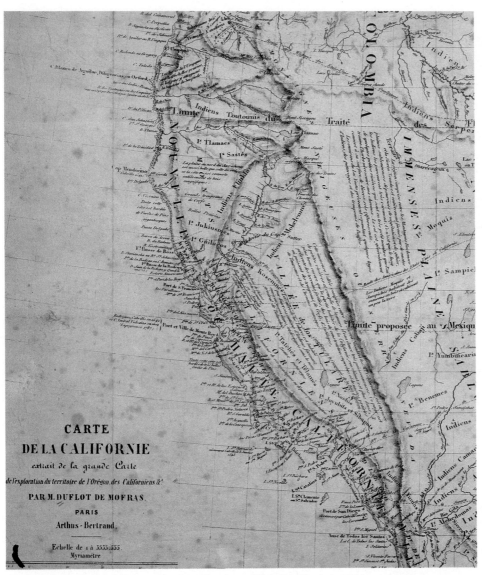

*The Eugene Duflot de Mofras map of California, published in Paris in 1844 as part of a two-volume work containing the Frenchman's observations made in California and Oregon during 1841–42. The map included the first known charting of San Simeon Bay, which Mofras visited along with other parts of Jose de Jesus Pico's Rancho Piedra Blanca.*

San Simeon was already beginning to emerge from the sleepy isolation of the Spanish-Mexican era when George Hearst arrived in 1865 and bought some 30,000 acres of Piedra Blanca, the first of many parcels he would buy from Pico and other owners. More than 17,000 acres of Pico's great ranch had been sold as early as 1854, and within the last few years other newcomers had gained a foothold in the district. This modest population boom resulted in a stepping-up of schooner traffic at San Simeon Bay. Dairying, agriculture, and ranching were beginning to replace the antiquated Mexican cattle industry the drought had destroyed; all depended heavily on San Simeon shipping for connections with distant markets. The most colorful new venture was the shore-whaling operation that had been started a year before Hearst's arrival by Joseph Clark. For the next thirty years Clark and his crews would pursue a majestic quarry, the California gray whales that annually migrate from the Gulf of Alaska to Baja California and back again, passing close to San Simeon each way. Mining was also becoming important in the nearby Santa Lucias, and like the other new enterprises it was almost wholly dependent on shipping connections through San Simeon Bay.

Cinnabar was discovered in the nearby hills in the early 1860s, and in 1871 locals began to speak of the Pine Mountain Lode. Four years later in the wilds south of Big Sur the Los Burros Mining District was formed, its southern boundary marked by San Carpoforo Creek—"Sankypoky," as some of the crusty miners called it. George Hearst had gone through a crusty period himself, first in the lead mines of his native Missouri and then in the gold fields of California. But the fabulous Comstock Lode stood between George's rough-and-ready days and his new role as the Baron of San Simeon. Evidently he was content to let the local mining rush run its course while he concentrated on developing his portion of Piedra Blanca. Five generations earlier George Hearst's forebears had left Scotland for the new world; their

*An abandoned stone bridge visible from Highway 1 marks Arroyo del Padre Juan, the boundary line between Rancho Piedra Blanca to the left and Rancho San Simeon to the right.*

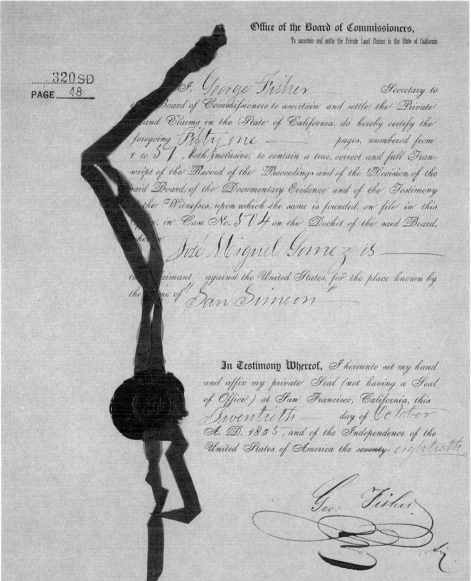

*By the time California became a state in 1850, Rancho San Simeon belonged to Jose Miguel Gomez. His claim of 4,469 acres was confirmed in 1855 and patented in 1865. But neighboring Rancho Piedra Blanca was not patented until 1876 — too late to save Jose de Jesus Pico from ruin.*

descendants moved through Virginia, through the Carolinas, and eventually to the far western frontier called Missouri, steadfastly maintaining a passion for land and for the matchless sense of freedom that possessing it could bring. George could afford to pursue his destiny far beyond his forefathers' dreams, and his son—representing the seventh generation of Hearsts in America—would be able to do so even further.

The 1870s saw George Hearst develop and expand his San Simeon interests mightily. He modernized the wharfage at San Simeon Bay, spent a small fortune on ranch improvements, built a handsome two-story Italianate mansion, and added more Piedra Blanca and adjoining acres to his holdings, along with portions of Rancho Santa Rosa south of Cambria.

George Hearst and his family didn't overlook the prospects for leisure in their new ranch kingdom. The era of excursioning and camping on the imperial scale had dawned; what could be more appropriate than the Hearsts' regarding Piedra Blanca as their exclusive answer to the hot springs, the natural wonderlands, the sumptuous resorts that the rich were frequenting? Remoteness and privacy they had aplenty, and with the Pacific on the one side and the Santa Lucias on the other the scenery filled the bill perfectly. The favorite destination was the long ridge the government mapmakers would one day name Lone Tree Hill for the solitary clump of laurels at its west end—the same ridge that W. R. Hearst would later christen La Cuesta Encantada. But to the Hearst family in those early years the spot was simply Camp Hill, and

*Shore whaling flourished along the California coast in the latter part of the nineteenth century. At San Simeon Bay, seventeen whales made up an average year's catch; but one season Captain Joseph Clark and his crew brought in twenty-three, an impressive number for a shore-based operation.*

*Built in the 1870s as part of George Hearst's improvement of his San Simeon holdings, the ranch house, as it is simply called, is carefully maintained by the Hearst Corporation today—a prime specimen of nineteenth-century residential architecture.*

*George Hearst (1820–91).*

*Phoebe Apperson Hearst (1842–1919).*

there they led a life of splendid rusticity. Memories and traditions naturally grew out of the halcyon days of Camp Hill. William Randolph Hearst later quipped that he had ascended the 1,600-foot slope by hanging on to the tail of his pony. The most endearing tradition of all was the Hearsts' use of unpretentious condiment bottles on the camp tables, a tradition that W. R. Hearst kept alive in the great mansion he eventually built on the site of the beloved vacation spot.

In the late 1880s George Hearst became a United States Senator. He and his wife, Phoebe, moved from San Francisco to appropriately regal quarters at 1400 New Hampshire Avenue in Washington D.C., and their son began his legendary publishing career with his first newspaper, the San Francisco *Examiner*. With George's death in 1891, Phoebe's increasing devotion to philanthropy and travel, and W. R.'s move to New York in the mid-Nineties, San Simeon, Piedra Blanca, and Camp Hill faded into the background. Phoebe Hearst eventually returned to California and her country estate near Pleasanton, the *Hacienda del Pozo de Verona;* her trips to the old family ranch became rare, though she did add more acreage to her late husband's holdings. Even her son appears to have passed many a year without visiting San Simeon— business, politics, and a family of his own kept him in the east most of the time. What trips he did make to his home state revolved around his San Francisco and Los Angeles newspapers and his mother's home in Pleasanton.

*William Randolph Hearst (1863–1951).*

*The era of whaling and commercial shipping is a distant memory at placid San Simeon Bay today, and so are the days when W. R. Hearst brought building supplies and art works in by water. But fishermen and other mariners still rely on the sheltered harbor for protection from the prevailing northwesterlies.*

*Phoebe Hearst's Hacienda del Pozo de Verona was an architectural foreshadowing of San Simeon. The estate took its name from the pozo 'well' that was acquired in Italy by Mrs. Hearst's son in the 1890s. Hearst sold the Hacienda after his mother's death and removed the wellhead to San Simeon, where it can be seen today next to Casa del Mar.*

*Front page of the San Francisco* Daily Examiner *on the first day of young W. R. Hearst's proprietorship—March 4, 1887. The name was soon shortened to the* Examiner, *and "Monarch of the Dailies" was added to the masthead. Hearst later branched out to New York, Chicago, Boston, and other big cities across the country. By 1919 he could count a dozen daily papers among his varied holdings and, by the 1930s, more than twice that number. Hearst broke into the periodical field in 1903 with* Motor. *Another early property was* Hearst's Magazine, *acquired in 1911 and merged with* Cosmopolitan *in 1925. The work of Maxfield Parrish and other famous illustrators frequently appeared on the covers of this and other magazines in the Hearst chain.*

"I love this ranch. It is wonderful. I love
the sea, and I love the mountains and the
hollows in the hills, and the shady places
in the creeks, and the fine old oaks . . . ."
—*William Randolph Hearst
to his mother, c. 1917*

When the Great War broke out in Europe, Hearst, who was entering his fifties, found time for longer trips to California. About 1917, as one of his sons later recalled, the publisher took his family down to San Simeon after the customary stopover at Grandmother Hearst's; perhaps plans for building on the ranch were already beginning to turn in his mind. At any rate the great days of Camp Hill were enthusiastically revived. In a letter to his mother, Hearst revealed how truly rugged a San Simeon outing could be, and he concluded by singing the praises of the future setting and backdrop for La Cuesta Encantada:

*We have been up to the Sancho Pojo and rode from there up the Coast for ten or twelve miles. We went last night up to Pat Garrity's and camped. This morning the two youngest woke us all up at half past four.*

*We had breakfast and then came down to the Arroyo la Cruz and went in swimming in a big pool, first the children, then the girls, and finally the men.*

*We are back in our regular camp at the top of the hill now, tired and sleepy on account of those kids. I love this ranch. It is wonderful. I love the sea, and I love the mountains and the hollows in the hills, and the shady places in the creeks, and the fine old oaks, and even the hot brushy hillsides —full of quail, and the canyons full of deer. It's a wonderful place. I would rather spend a month here than any place in the world. And as a sanitarium! Mother, it has Nauheim, Karlsbad, Vichy, Wiesbaden, French Lick, Sartoga and every other so-called health resort beaten a nautical mile. . . .*

Little did Hearst realize how close he was to fulfilling the dream he conveyed between the lines of that letter.

Phoebe Apperson Hearst, a victim of the influenza epidemic that swept the country at the end of World War I, died in 1919; William Randolph Hearst inherited Piedra Blanca and life for him, for his family, for San Simeon, and, in a sense, for the entire world would never be quite the same again.

*Day's end over San Simeon Point.*

"The work in front of "C" is going to be a grand success . . . ." –*Julia Morgan to W. R. Hearst, January 17, 1921*

# THE DREAM
# UNFOLDS

Even the most ambitious dreams go through an uncertain, formative period before they are transformed into realities. William Randolph Hearst's dream for San Simeon was no exception, despite his previous experience as a builder in the grand manner. Incredible as it may sound, his first consultation with his architect, Julia Morgan, indicated nothing more than a desire to have "something that would be more comfortable" than his vacation retreat on Camp Hill had been. "I get tired of going up there and camping in tents," Hearst told Miss Morgan . "I'm getting a little old for that." Perhaps, he said, it would be nice to build a single structure of the type called a bungalow.

Could Hearst really have been that unconscious of his destiny when he approached Julia Morgan in the spring of 1919? Perhaps he could pay only passing attention to the prospect of developing San Simeon; perhaps he was preoccupied with the settlement of his late mother's estate and was therefore content to meditate a while on the unrivaled possibilities that lay before him. Whatever the explanation, he was not long in rallying to the cause. Within two or three weeks of that first consultation with Julia

Morgan, Hearst began to think about San Simeon in regal terms, and before the year was out he was ready to plunge into the new venture with his characteristic zeal.

Julia Morgan was ready too. Easily the most accomplished woman in the history of American architecture— and for that matter one of this country's most accomplished architects whether man *or* woman— Morgan was approaching the mid-point in a career that began shortly after 1900 and spanned the first half of the twentieth century. Known both as a versatile problem-solver and as an unselfish "client's architect," Morgan was a wise choice on Hearst's part, as the complexities of the San Simeon job would continually prove.

The choice was based on a good deal of precedent. Hearst met Morgan in 1902, shortly after the young woman returned from the renowned Beaux-Arts architectural school in Paris, and while she was working on additions to Phoebe Hearst's Pleasanton estate, the *Hacienda del Pozo de Verona.* In 1906 Morgan refurbished Hearst's *Examiner* building in San Francisco after the great earthquake and fire; six years later Hearst retained her to design

another *Examiner* building, this time in Los Angeles. And about 1918 Hearst asked Morgan to plan a villa in Sausalito, across the bay from San Francisco—a project that never materialized, because Hearst soon focused his attention on San Simeon.

Many recognize Hearst as one of the greatest romantics who ever lived, but few understand that Julia Morgan was highly idealistic and romantic herself. With one arm she embraced the modernism that was coming of age around her; with the other she clung to a past that was too sustaining to relinquish. In Hearst she had a client—a patron, he might better be called—who mirrored her far-reaching sympathy for the past, particularly for the Middle Ages. Morgan revered the medieval ideal of the master builder, who directed the efforts of stonecutters, masons, glasers, and other artisans as they erected a cathedral or other great building. San Simeon and other commissions from Hearst gave her the opportunity to realize that ideal.

How did W. R. Hearst and Julia Morgan decide what work was to be done? Which of them called the shots? Did Hearst know what he was doing or did Morgan have to point the way? Over the years questions like these have been asked repeatedly, but only recently have some of them been answered satisfactorily. A long-standing, disheartening myth held that Morgan burned all her records when she retired, sparing not a single scrap. She did in fact dispose of part of her office files and years of accumulated architectural drawings, but, as luck would have it, some of her choicest records—which included correspondence with Hearst and others on the subject of San Simeon—were not destroyed. Since 1980 the material has been available to researchers through California

*By the end of 1919, William Randolph Hearst's dream for San Simeon had expanded greatly, but he had yet to think of his newly inherited estate as more than a vacation retreat. By 1927, however, he could write to his architect, Julia Morgan, "I had no idea when we began to build the ranch that I would be here so much or that the construction would be so important." Soon after that, San Simeon became Hearst's primary residence.*

*Left: Millicent Willson Hearst peers into a Byzantine font in the courtyard of the middle house. In 1921, Mrs. Hearst gave old Camp Hill a new name,* Las Estrellas; *but she and her husband later found that a ranch near Paso Robles already bore a similar name. In 1924, the hilltop was rechristened* La Cuesta Encantada.

*Although she grew up in Oakland, California, Julia Morgan was, like W. R. Hearst, a native of San Francisco. After attending the University of California in the 1890s and the Beaux-Arts in Paris at the turn of the century, Morgan returned to the Bay Area and soon became one of California's leading architects. Her commissions ranged up and down the state and occasionally farther afield. She died in 1957 at the age of eighty-five, having designed hundreds of buildings in addition to those for William Randolph Hearst.*

*Above: Miss Morgan during her student days in Paris, c. 1900.*

*An early study by Julia Morgan of a "bungalow" for San Simeon—date unknown, but probably late spring or early summer of 1919. The correspondence between Hearst and Morgan indicates that, by mid-summer at least, they had begun to think of an "architectural group" comprised of a main central building and outlying "houses." Before long, "bungalow" virtually disappeared from their terminology.*

Polytechnic State University in San Luis Obispo, which, as luck would also have it, is only fifty miles south of Hearst Castle. Not surprisingly, the Julia Morgan Collection has already revolutionized previous thinking.

The San Simeon correspondence reveals that center stage belonged to William Randolph Hearst throughout his association with Julia Morgan, as well it should have, since his grandiose dream, his aspirations, his flights of whimsical fancy, his dynastic wealth fired the epic project at nearly every turn. For the protagonist Hearst, Morgan played the finest supporting role of her career. Their relationship was thoroughly congenial and at the same time professional. To the very end of their long collaboration they addressed each other in a somewhat old-fashioned but always dignified way as "Mr. Hearst" and "Miss Morgan."

"The main thing at the ranch is the view."
—*W. R. Hearst to Julia Morgan,*
   *October 25, 1919*

In 1919 Hearst lived in New York, and Morgan in San Francisco. Consequently consultation-by-mail proved absolutely imperative, allowing Hearst to stay as involved as he liked to be. From the outset, therefore, the Hearst-Morgan correspondence played a critical, decisive part in the planning and execution of the work at San Simeon.

The earliest surviving letters, dating from the summer of 1919, when the Hearsts were in residence at the hilltop campsite, draw the curtains back on a scenario already in progress. By then a few months had passed since Hearst proposed a single bungalow structure, and a considerably bolder plan had emerged, a plan for a group of buildings that would revolve around a towered main structure in a manner reminiscent of a Spanish hill town. Hearst had come a long way since his original bungalow proposal, but his dream was still somewhat embryonic. Surely he was thinking of much simpler structures than we see today

when he told Julia Morgan that he wanted the main central unit built first and ready for occupancy by the following summer. The outlying, smaller buildings, according to this plan, could be started afterwards and could be ready by the summer of 1921. How they must have smiled if ever in later years they paused to recall that first summer!

As soon as Hearst returned to New York in the fall of 1919, he took up the question of the smaller, encircling structures. The exact topographical placement of the trio that would become known simply as "the houses" had to be determined, as did a great many other details like size, scale, floor plan, and ornamentation. Three thousand miles away from something that was becoming more fascinating with every passing day, Hearst depended on his correspondence with Julia Morgan to keep him in close touch. In one letter he reminded her to take good advantage of the natural beauty of the region, stating succinctly that "The main thing at the ranch is

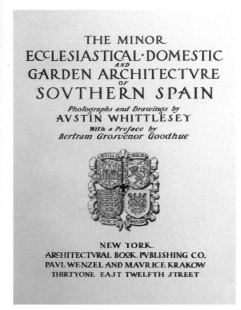

THE MINOR
ECCLESIASTICAL·DOMESTIC
*AND*
GARDEN ARCHITECTVRE
*OF*
SOVTHERN SPAIN

*Photographs and Drawings by*
AVSTIN WHITTLESEY
*With a Preface by*
*Bertram Grosvenor Goodhue*

NEW YORK
ARCHITECTVRAL BOOK PVBLISHING CO.
PAVL WENZEL AND MAVRICE KRAKOW
THIRTYONE EAST TWELFTH STREET

*In December of 1919, Hearst sent Julia Morgan a copy of Austin Whittlesey's book on Spanish architecture. From it they derived inspiration for the arched loggia and the Moorish windows of House "C," the large marble fountain on the west side of the same building, and the flat-arch entrance to the main building. Additional motifs were taken from* Spanish Architecture of the Sixteenth Century *by Arthur Byne and Mildred Stapley.*

"... when we get the cottages built, we can lay out a plan of walks and flower beds or landscape features of some kind that will bring all the structures together into a harmonious whole." —*W. R. Hearst to Julia Morgan, December 21, 1919*

the view." In the same letter he informed her that he had decided to hold off on starting the main building until after the houses were completed, which he hoped would be in time for his next summer vacation.

The grandeur that even the smaller buildings would eventually embody, and the important role they would play in the overall architectural scheme, became more apparent as Hearst and Morgan compared notes. Before that first year was out, Hearst could write, "We refer to them as little houses, but they are not really little houses. They are only little as compared with the big central building." Concerning the placement of the houses, Hearst emphasized that they shouldn't be situated too far down the side of the hill lest the main building seem "ashamed of them." He went on to say in their behalf:

*They could be treated that way if they were servants' quarters or out-buildings of small importance; but as they are dwelling houses of consequence, and very pretty*

*buildings, I think they should be brought more into the general composition, and treated as attractive features of it.*

He concluded by saying that landscape design would eventually unify all the structures, producing a "harmonious whole."

Not until February of 1920 did actual construction begin on the houses. In the meantime Hearst and Morgan weighed the question of architectural style and made some important choices that, to a greater or lesser degree, would influence most of the work at San Simeon for more than two decades. At least as early as September of 1919 they considered the Cathedral of Santa Maria la Mayor in Ronda, Spain, as an inspiration for the main building. By then, they had apparently decided that the historical character of the San Simeon group should be Hispanic, but the particular type of Spanish architecture was still to be resolved. Hearst discussed the matter at length on the last day of the year:

*The Panama-California Exposition in San Diego (1915–16) launched the Spanish Colonial Revival, an architectural style that took California by storm. But W. R. Hearst and Julia Morgan preferred their own interpretation of the Spanish heritage — something "a little different than other people are doing out in California," as Hearst modestly put it. They selected the "Southern Spanish Renaissance" for San Simeon; from that point of departure, Hearst and Morgan eventually forged a style uniquely its own — a style that has successfully resisted typecasting ever since.*

*I have thought a great deal over whether to make this whole group of buildings Baroc, in the Eighteenth Century style, or Renaissance.*

*It is quite a problem. I started out with the Baroc in mind, as nearly all the Spanish architecture in America is of that character. . . .*

*If we should decide on this style, I would at least want to depart from the very crude and rude examples of it that we have in our early California Spanish architecture.*

*The Mission at Santa Barbara is doubtless the highest example of this California architecture, and yet it is very bare and almost clumsy to my mind.*

*The best things I have seen in this Spanish Baroc are at the San Diego Exposition. . . .*

*I understand that the San Diego Exposition stuff is largely reproductions from the best examples in Mexico and South America, and that we could not go to a better source to get the most agreeable specimens of this style.*

*This style at its best is sufficiently satisfactory, though in our early California architecture it seems to me too primitive, and in many examples I have seen in Mexico so elaborate as to be objectionable.*

*Between these two extremes, however, there are good examples and I think the San Diego Exposition affords the best.*

*. . . The alternative is to build this group of buildings in the Renaissance style of Southern Spain. We picked out the towers of the Church of Ronda. I suppose they are Renaissance or else transitional, and they have some Gothic feeling; but a Renaissance decoration, particularly that of the very southern part of Spain, would harmonize well with them.*

*The Renaissance of Northern Spain seems to me very hard, while the Renaissance of Southern Spain is much softer and more graceful.*

*We get very beautiful decoration for the central building and for the cottages out of this Southern Spanish Renaissance style, and I think that would, in the main, be the best period for interior decoration.*

*The trouble would be, I suppose, that it has no historic association with California, or rather with the Spanish architecture in California.*

*. . . But after all, would it not be better to do something a little different than other people are doing out in California as long as we do not do anything incongruous?*

Julia Morgan's reply showed how productive their correspondence could be and how she felt completely free to disagree in the best interests of the project, something Hearst often encouraged her to do:

*Two years ago work took me down to San Diego very frequently and I know*

*the buildings well. The composition and decoration are certainly very well handled indeed, but I question whether this type of decoration would not seem too heavy and clumsy on our buildings, because while the Exposition covers acres with its buildings, we have a comparatively small group, and it would seem that they should charm by their detail rather than overwhelm by more or less clumsy exuberance.*

*I feel just as you do about the early California Mission style as being too primitive to be gone back to and copied. . . . As I wrote you in my last*

*Santa Maria la Mayor, Ronda, Spain.*

"Am sending you copies of the original approved studies and two new studies for your own house . . . I like the outside steps and little lower terrace immensely. The first sketch would look as suggested in the group sketch that shows the 'Ronda' motif for the main building." —*Julia Morgan to W. R. Hearst, January 5, 1920*

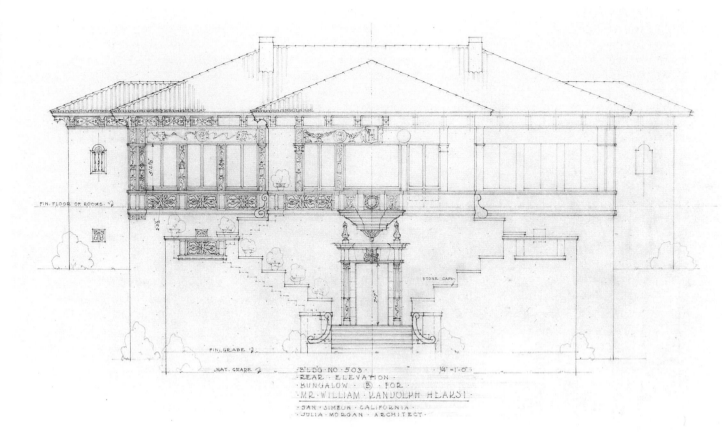

·B'LDG·NO·503·
·REAR·ELEVATION·
·BUNGALOW·(B)·FOR·
·MR·WILLIAM·RANDOLPH·HEARST·
·SAN·SIMEON·CALIFORNIA·
·JULIA·MORGAN·ARCHITECT·

"... all the little houses are stunning and the lightly different treatment makes them very attractive. I think you are right about House B. Please complete them before I can think up any more changes."
—*W. R. Hearst to Julia Morgan, March 18, 1920*

*letter, I believe we could get something really very beautiful by using the combination of Ronda Towers and the Sevilla doorway. . . .*

As soon as Hearst heard from Morgan, he cabled back, "Our definite decision in favor of the Renaissance makes it unnecessary to go into the San Diego Exposition stuff at all." The plural "Our," it should be noted, referred to Hearst and his wife, Millicent, who shared much of her husband's enthusiasm for San Simeon in these early years. (It was Millicent Hearst, for instance, who began calling the hilltop *Las Estrellas*, a name used until the more dramatic *La Cuesta Encantada* was chosen in 1924.)

"It was necessary to provide board, lodging and transportation in order to get men in any of the trades, crafts or even plain labor. The cost of temporary shacks, tents, bedding, kitchen and dining outfits etc. has been heavy, but these are an asset . . . . The camp is run on somewhat less than a dollar a day per man, which is a good record as there are no complaints as to food. The chef says he is the most important man on the mountain . . . ."—*Julia Morgan to W. R. Hearst, May 19, 1920*

The selection of an architectural style was not the only consideration. All the while Hearst and Morgan had their hands full with practical, utilitarian matters. San Simeon was actually more isolated in 1920 than it had been years earlier. After the Southern Pacific rails linked San Luis Obispo with the rest of California, the use of San Simeon Bay had fallen off sharply. No coastal steamers had called there regularly since 1915, and the old pier from George Hearst's era had deteriorated. The alternative of using the narrow coast road up through Morro Bay and Cambria was even less attractive, especially during the rainy season. Julia Morgan had already had difficulty getting building materials to the job site, and the coming of winter compounded her problems.

Morgan also had trouble assembling an adequate labor force, despite Hearst's authorizing her to pay premium wages as an inducement. Unsettled post-war conditions in the building industry were mostly to blame; the new decade had dawned, but the Twenties boom was still in the future. Work on the three houses proceeded nonetheless; it soon became apparent, however, that it would be impossible to complete them in time for the Hearsts' summer visit. In April of 1920 the situation remained largely the same, as Morgan reported to Hearst in New York:

*The shortages of every kind of material and workmen out here is incredible, from draughtsmen to window glass inclusive. . . . I had to take one of the modelers up to San Simeon this week and convince him that it was a "lovely place" and then have him telephone from there back to the shop that I was veracious, before the cast-cement crew would agree to go up. . . .*

*You were evidently right about getting a country trained builder, for I do not believe we could have held a city man. The San Francisco men sent down on the "bonus" plan have nearly all come back, one turned back at San Simeon, some got to the top of the hill and did not unpack, and some stayed a week or more. They all agreed that the living conditions, money and food were all right, but they "didn't like feeling so far away from things." Mr. Washburn is picking up "country men" as fast as he can. . . .*

"Expect you have had a devil of a time getting the houses as far along as they are—Will appreciates your efforts—& difficulties surmounted & realizes it was no picnic." —*Orrin Peck to Julia Morgan, May, 1920*

*Julia Morgan sketches while Hearst looks on—fall of 1920 in the courtyard of House "B," the eventual* Casa del Monte.

"Tile is gradually arriving for steps of various terraces, but the output of the kilns is as small as ever and it is coming in spoonfuls, as it did for the house friezes. Some of it is lovely in color."—*Julia Morgan to W. R. Hearst, June 28, 1921*

*One of a pair of door grilles made for House "C" by Ed Trinkkeller, a German who produced a variety of decorative ironwork details in his Los Angeles studio. Folklore has it that the little heads represent master craftsmen associated with the San Simeon job; one of the portraits is said to be of Trinkkeller himself.*

"With a small crew, Vanderloo has done a very fine creditable amount of work . . . while it sounds simple to reproduce antiques, in reality it is a long job as the design has to be reversed."—*Julia Morgan to W. R. Hearst, January 5, 1921*

One of superintendent Washburn's new "country men" was Frank Souza, who became construction foreman and stayed on for many years. Other locals also began long, productive careers. But there was always a need for highly skilled "city men"; and San Simeon's fine wood carving, wrought iron, plaster and cast stone decoration, tile work, and other contemporary efforts are sure indications that Hearst and Morgan finally succeeded in recruiting the necessary talent.

Theo Van der Loo was the first master craftsman to work at San Simeon, coming down from Oakland to get the cast stone decoration under way on the three houses; more than twenty years later his son John would still be working on sections of the main building. From New York came Frank Humrich and his crew; among them was a Hungarian named Frank Gyorgy, who would stay on into the 1930s and whose versatility as an architectural decorator would prove indispensable. Other specialists never relinquished their "city man" status, since they could work more effectively out of their established studios. In San Francisco Jules Suppo was kept busy for several years carving ornamental woodwork. Fellow San Franciscans F. M. Lorenz, an equally skilled woodcarver, and L. Cardini, a marble sculptor, also turned out large quantities of work in their studios. In Los Angeles, meanwhile, worked Ed Trinkkeller, a German who specialized in decorative ironwork and who had worked for Hearst and Morgan on the *Examiner* building in 1912.

Still other names like Camille Solon, John Pelligrini, J. L. Divet, and Val Georges can be mentioned—but many more cannot, because they have been lost in the maze of historical details surrounding the Castle. Whether remembered or forgotten, the workers—from the laborers on Souza's concrete crew to the artisans of Jules Suppo's stature—had as much to do with San Simeon's becoming a reality as Hearst and Morgan did. They have rightly been called the unsung heroes of the hill.

"As telegraphed last night, Las Estrellas has had a thorough trying out climatically this winter and really has come through beautifully on the whole."—*Julia Morgan to W. R. Hearst, January 26, 1922*

*Colored drawing of the main building, c. May 1922. The penciled lines along the bottom are Hearst's: "I think there should be ten feet more width between the towers for the central gabled building. I think this will help rather than hurt the front elevation and it will be much better inside for the big assembly room giving that 85 ft length, and clearing the tapestries from above the doors into the refectory."*

*The prototype for S. Miletin's 1920's copy of the fountain on the west side of House "C" (Plate 90 in Austin Whittlesey's* Minor Ecclesiastical, Domestic and Garden Architecture of Southern Spain, *1917).*

"Would like shaft of C fountain to be greyish white marble with polished finish to match Moorish columns but lions more reddish like Verona marble. Will put bronze figure on top of this shaft . . . ."
—*W. R. Hearst to Julia Morgan, May 6, 1922 (from a telegram sent while eastbound through Truckee, California)*

*Surviving sketches and drawings by Julia Morgan and her staff range from the rough to the very refined, and from tiny scraps of paper to full-scale sheets several feet long. The smaller ones especially are often nostalgic and charming, as typified by this colored-pencil sketch on tracing tissue, c. 1922.*

In 1920 the houses were still incomplete, and so the Hearsts spent a final season in their nearby tents. It was not until the summer of 1921 that the family used the houses for the first time, even though they were far from finished. Because the Hearsts passed up California the following year in favor of a European vacation, Julia Morgan had until the summer of 1923 to conclude this first major phase of the job. Even then a number of loose ends remained, but at least the Hearsts' tents could now be dispensed with for good.

By 1923 the focal point had shifted to what would eventually be named *Casa Grande,* the huge main building that had been started the summer before and that now loomed over the houses as a rough gray hulk. By the end of 1923 the cathedral-like structure had been raised to the third and fourth floors—the "big pour," Morgan called it—and by 1924 it had been extended high enough to reveal the Ronda-style towers that Hearst and Morgan had decided upon back in 1919.

Despite his protracted absence from San Simeon, Hearst kept abreast of the work with his customary thoroughness. The project had long

since assumed a complexity that characterized all his endeavors, a multiplicity that challenged his vibrant imagination and nearly foolproof memory. Countless architectural questions along with more prosaic matters ranging from roadwork and fencing to water and

*The view from Chinese Hill—summer of 1923. The houses are well along, as are first-generation pathways and retaining walls on the lower slopes. Most of these small-scale outdoor details were replaced or, in some instances, completely covered over by larger architectural features during the next ten years. The pencil lines in the foreground—probably in Julia Morgan's hand—hint at proposed work near the eventual site of the Neptune Pool. Behind House "B," the main building begins to rear its reinforced concrete mass to the sky.*

power supplies had been submitted to him by Julia Morgan and, as often, had been submitted to her by him. Now a man of sixty, Hearst would live almost thirty more years, through half of which he would enjoy vigorous health. Surely with the houses virtually completed and the main building well under way, his mind was humming with visions of grandeur, his spirit animated by the great enterprise unfolding before him.

One pursuit that had kept Hearst raptly attentive since 1919 was the collecting of art, especially art for San Simeon. Hearst had been a familiar figure in the art world since the turn of the century, often collecting for pleasure, along with other auction-room sportsmen of the day. But San Simeon gave him a particular focus, a particular need. Once Hearst chose a theme for the estate that first winter, he immediately began to collect complimentary items through the New York art market. At the opening of the 1919-20 sales season, New York's galleries were piled high with hand-me-downs of every description from the ancestral collections of war-ruined Europe. Even more furnishings, more

objects of art, more architectural elements would become available to Americans during the Twenties boom. The diversity and abundance would prove nearly inexhaustible—a bonanza that history timed perfectly for W. R. Hearst.

Hearst followed the art market firsthand in the 1920s, often spending several hours a week in the auction rooms and galleries. A mighty inheritance along with the need to amass a bounty of decorative objects drove him to collect on a level rivaling the great art dealers of the period. Hearst became a virtual Lord Duveen or French & Compay, stockpiling art

*All the while ranch work continued on Piedra Blanca. Hearst planned to raise commercial farm crops on his property, but as time went on beef cattle became the chief concern of the Hearst Ranch and remain so today.*

and architectural works in grandiose array for his new dream house at San Simeon. He covered the European market at the same time through agents in London and on the Continent; although New York had come to dominate the art market, there were still prizes to be bagged abroad, choice things that might never find their way across the Atlantic otherwise.

By March of 1920, Hearst had accumulated enough material to fill a freight car, which he dispatched to California in time for Julia Morgan to incorporate some of the architectural pieces into the three houses. From then until the late 1930s, several "cars," as these rail shipments were designated, were sent to the west coast each year. For Morgan they seemed in the early going like Christmas one moment and a burden the next. In 1921, writing to the antiquarians Arthur Byne and Mildred Stapley Byne—who were soon to be purveyors of Spanish art to Hearst direct from their home base in Madrid—Morgan described the nature of Hearst's collecting:

*So far we have received from him, to incorporate in the new buildings, some twelve or thirteen carloads of antiques, brought from the ends of the earth and from prehistoric down to late Empire in period, the majority, however, being of Spanish origin.*

*They comprise vast quantities of tables, beds, armoires, secretaires, all kinds of cabinets, polychrome church statuary, columns, door frames, carved doors in all stages of repair and disrepair, over-altars, reliquaries, lanterns, iron grille doors, window grilles, votive candlesticks, torcheres, all kinds of chairs in quantity, six or seven well heads . . . I don't see myself where we are ever going to use half suitably, but I find that the idea is to try things out and if they are not satisfactory, discard them for the next thing that comes that promises better. There is interest and charm coming gradually into play. . . .*

*Hearst began to collect art steadily in the 1890's. But until 1919, his interest in Spanish and Italian works —the predominant types at San Simeon —lay relatively fallow. In 1913, for example, he acquired Jean Leon Gerome's* Bonaparte in Egypt *through the sale of the Borden Collection; at the same auction Hearst bought a pair of Graeco-Phoenician gold bracelets. The Bonaparte picture, one of two by Gerome that were later hung in the Celestial Suite, may well have reminded Hearst of his trip to Europe in 1879 when, at the age of sixteen, he sat for his portrait bust in Gerome's Paris studio.*

*Architectural collecting was one of Hearst's greatest interests. At his height he was unsurpassed in the acquisition of columns, doorways, mantelpieces, ceilings, paneled rooms, and, in several instances, entire buildings. This painted ceiling from Italy, acquired in 1924, was installed in the Doge's Suite two years later.*

*Hearst inherited real estate and mining properties when his mother died in 1919; he also inherited the renowned art collection that Phoebe Hearst had assembled over a forty-year period. One of his mother's treasures was* The Encounter, *a seventeenth-century tapestry that hangs in the arched loft of the Refectory.*

As Hearst's buying became more systematic and as Morgan became more adept at working with his acquisitions, the art collection assumed greater importance for both of them. By 1924 Morgan revealed to Arthur Byne how much she had come to share Hearst's ever-expanding dream when she wrote, "I have developed an absorptive capacity that seems ungodly when I stop and reflect."

Hearst and Morgan became increasingly concerned about the quality of the art works they were using at San Simeon. In March of 1925 Morgan wrote to Arthur Byne again, telling him that if he could get "finer and more important things they would be welcome." Two years later Hearst addressed the same issue in one of the most significant passages in his extensive correspondence with Julia Morgan:

*A great many very fine things will be arriving for the ranch –some of them have already arrived.*

*They are for the most part of a much higher grade than we have had heretofore. In fact, I have decided to buy only the finest things for the ranch from now on, and we will probably weed out some of our less desirable articles.*

*I had no idea when we began to build the ranch that I would be here so much or that the construction itself would be so important. Under the present circumstances, I see no reason why the ranch should not be a museum of the best things I can secure. . . .*

This was Hearst's first reference to San Simeon as a museum, but in all likelihood he and Morgan had already considered it one, perhaps for quite some time. In any event, they set their sights accordingly, prompting a Morgan associate, Walter Steilberg, to speak of them years later as "long distance dreamers" who were "looking way, way ahead."

The museum idea had a practical, immediate side, too. With Hearst's life revolving more and more around San Simeon, and with his reputation as the perfect host firmly established in New York and Hollywood, why shouldn't Hearst make his hilltop palace as magnificent as possible? Why shouldn't he create a backdrop that would dazzle and amaze today and that would enrich and inspire tomorrow? Hearst, the great dreamer, the consummate showman, knew that if he proceeded accordingly he would not be playing to an empty house.

*A pair of giltwood* **putti** *from a Venetian doorway dance a jig after arriving at San Simeon in 1920.*

*Right: An undercurrent of classicism runs through much of the San Simeon collection, especially outdoors, where Hearst displayed copies of ancient works as well as important originals. Here, a copy of the* Crouching Venus *joins ranks with Spanish ironwork and glazed tiles in the courtyard of the smallest house, Casa del Monte.*

*In February of 1927, with La Cuesta Encantada on the verge of its heyday, Hearst wrote Julia Morgan, "I see no reason why the ranch should not be a museum of the best things I can secure." A year later he acquired what some consider to be San Simeon's finest painting—Adriaen Ysenbrandt's* Madonna and Child with Two Angels, *a Flemish work of the sixteenth century.*

*By the mid-1920s, San Simeon boasted yet another marvel —a collection of exotic animals, many of which roamed freely in a 2,000-acre preserve below La Cuesta Encantada.*

# HEYDAY AND TWILIGHT

In the mid-1920s William Randolph Hearst spent more time at his California barony—his ranch, as he and his friends called it—than he had before, and he would continue to spend more time there from then on. In a lavish 1931 feature entitled "Hearst at Home," *Fortune* magazine noted that Mr. Hearst had spent 204 days in residence at San Simeon during 1930, something that would have been unimaginable ten years earlier. (One half of the remaining days in 1930 Hearst had devoted to a European excursion; the other half he had divided between New York and Los Angeles.) By 1930 La Cuesta Encantada had become Hearst's favorite and most frequented address and would remain so until the outbreak of World War II. The estate had also become a favorite of the many guests who had enjoyed Hearst's kingly hospitality, if only for a fleeting weekend. For them, La Cuesta Encantada was a wonderland that fully lived up to its name.

Hearst was an indulgent host, even during the old camping days. Camp Hill consisted of a main dining tent and a cluster of smaller sleeping tents; that arrangement, along with traditions like the screening of movies

under the spacious California sky, helped cast the die for the marvels to come. Julia Morgan knew from the outset that, by replacing the tents with permanent buildings, Hearst intended to accommodate and entertain not only himself and his family but many others as well. A plan for two houses in addition to the Hearsts' own—plus a larger main building—made that intention plain to see. But the thought of providing for guests in the truly grand manner had yet to occur to either Hearst or Morgan. Like everything else in the San Simeon epic, the social history began modestly. A decade later the transformation was well along, and in its 1931 article *Fortune* could report that for most of the 204 days in 1930, Hearst had "kept the guest rooms fairly full, the court being in session." The article also mentioned that some of the recent guests had been as noteworthy as Winston Churchill, who visited San Simeon in September of 1929.

But the names of only a few guests who visited during the earliest years are known. Presumably those first guests were newspapermen and other business associates, family friends, theatrical and motion picture people, and others both renowned and obscure—a preface to the social makeup that is better documented from the mid-1920s on. One of the visitors in 1924, for example, was John Hylan, the mayor through whom Hearst exerted potent influence on the municipal affairs of New York City.

Socially speaking, the year of Hylan's stay was the beginning of a new era for San Simeon. Until 1924, Hearst's visits had usually been family activities that originated in New York, required a certain amount of planning, favored the summer months, and included only small groups of guests. But in 1924, his visits became more frequent, were often short trips made any time of year and often at the drop of a hat, and were inclined to favor Hollywood celebrities—those "wild movie people," as Hearst said to Julia Morgan.

Some big changes in Hearst's life made 1924 the turning point. The Hearsts had separated, and Mr. Hearst began spending much of his time in Los Angeles, where his Cosmopolitan Productions—featuring Marion Davies as the principal star—found a new home under the wing of Metro-Goldwyn-Mayer in Culver City. The Metro-Goldwyn-Mayer crowd included many of the Hollywood elite: Louis B. Mayer, Greta Garbo, John Gilbert, Norma Shearer, Irving Thalberg, Francis X. Bushman, and other luminaries of the day soon bestowed an aura of glamour on San Simeon that became legendary. Another notable from the silent era who journeyed up the coast to the fabulous new estate was Rudolph Valentino, whose death in 1926 denied him the experience of Hearst's kingdom in its prime.

*Marion Davies, veteran of the Ziegfeld Follies and nearly fifty motion pictures made in New York and Hollywood between 1917 and 1937. After she moved to California in 1924, her films were released through Metro-Goldwyn-Mayer and, during the last three years of her career, Warner Brothers.*

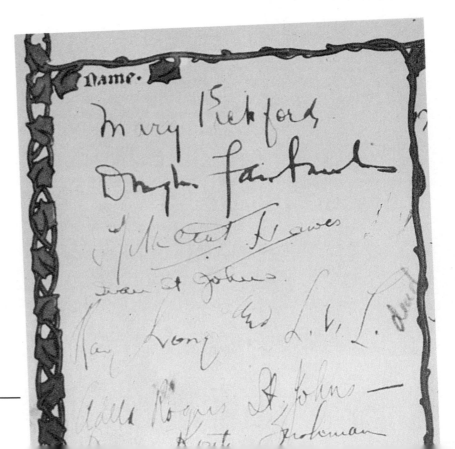

*Names both famous and obscure are found side by side throughout San Simeon's guest books, as in these entries from the summer of 1925.*

*Portrait of William Randolph Hearst by Metro-Goldwyn-Mayer photographer James Manatt.*

*Casa del Monte was the first of the houses to be completed. Casa del Sol and Casa del Mar required more time to finish, but by 1924 all three were ready for the full-scale use Hearst had been waiting to give them.*

*The main building was begun in 1922 while the outlying houses were still under construction. Part of Casa Grande was ready for use by the latter half of the Twenties, but other parts were not finished until the 1930s or even later. The towers were modified in 1926–27 to accommodate a Belgian carillon of bells, which was finally installed in 1932.*

The mid-1920s were still formative years in San Simeon's development; for that matter, the late 1920s and much of the 1930s would be too. In 1924 the three houses were virtually complete, but no more than temporary or improvised use could be made of the main building. Hearst himself maintained quarters in the largest house, by then named *Casa del Mar* 'House of the Sea.' The two others, *Casa del Sol* 'House of the Sun' and *Casa del Monte* 'House of the Mountain,' provided a total number of twelve bedrooms. If filled to capacity, along with whatever guest space may have been available in *Casa del Mar,* the houses could accommodate twenty-five or thirty people. When the main building came into use during the late Twenties, space opened up for fifteen to twenty more guests. But not until the 1930s would *Casa Grande* swell to the immense size we see today—a piecemeal evolution achieved mainly through the addition of more guest suites. Only then could Hearst accommodate a group of fifty or sixty—a number still far from the exaggerations, of which even *Fortune* was guilty in 1931, that blithely speak of 100 or 150 guests and that have become deeply ingrained in San Simeon mythology. But no one should be disappointed by the more realistic figures of one or two dozen guests with occasional increases to double that number or slightly more. With William Randolph Hearst and Marion Davies presiding over the court, ten or even five guests were enough to make San Simeon exciting and colorful.

From 1923 until 1927, W. R. Hearst stayed in Casa del Mar during his increasingly frequent visits to San Simeon; in the late Twenties he moved into the newly completed Gothic Suite in Casa Grande. Of the three houses, Casa del Mar is the most ornate, as exemplified by the main sitting room in the upper suite.

*From the time guests first saw it on Christmas Eve in 1925, through the heyday of the 1930s, and down to the present, the Assembly Room has been regarded as one of San Simeon's most magnificent interiors. Hearst fully intended that it should be so, placing the huge room strategically at the front of the main building, thus making it, in effect, the lobby of a grand hotel. Highlights include, from left to right, the Great Barney Mantel, a Flemish tapestry above Italian Renaissance choir stalls, another Flemish tapestry between two of Thorvaldsen's reliefs, and, on the large tables, bronze sculptures and silver candlesticks. The slipcovered furniture typifies Hearst's desire for modern-day comfort and informality in the midst of antiquarian splendor.*

Christmas Eve of 1925 has often been cited as San Simeon's "grand opening," the occasion on which W. R. Hearst "moved into the main building." But in 1925, as we can now see from the Hearst-Morgan correspondence and related evidence, nothing more than a preview of Casa Grande could have been offered, despite fairly steady construction for three years. True, a Hollywood group vacationed at the estate in December of 1925. The Refectory, the dining room in the main building, was not ready for use, but the group evidently gave Casa Grande a Christmas Eve housewarming anyway by dining in the huge Assembly Room. Within a few days, however, everyone returned to Los Angeles, Mr. Hearst and Miss Davies included. As to Hearst's occupying the main building, his private Gothic Suite would not be ready until the latter part of 1927; until then he would continue to stay in Casa del Mar during his intermittent visits.

Although the housewarming was somewhat premature, La Cuesta Encantada had much to offer in 1925, and perhaps we should review some of what Hearst and his guests may have seen during that Christmas celebration.

By the end of 1925 the overall project had progressed impressively in certain sections but less so in others. The three houses alone had been finished for at least a year. Up in Casa Grande, the smallest rooms—the second-floor Cloisters—were nearly finished, their antique Spanish ceilings having been installed during the summer. Half a floor below, the mezzanine Doge's Suite would be ready within six months. But the only other upstairs section that approached completion was the Library. The remaining upper areas—Hearst's own Gothic Suite and the tower-level Celestial Suite—were still far from finished at the end of 1925. The towers, in fact, had yet to be heightened to make way for the carillon bells, a major structural change that would not be undertaken until 1926.

*Earmarked for several years as the Music Room and still referred to by that name as late as 1933, the rough concrete space connecting the Morning Room and Theater was finally finished in 1934 as the Billiard Room. The long-standing plan for a Music Room—here or elsewhere in the main building—apparently was abandoned after that date.*

The ground floor was quite far along, having been started first. But the work was slowed by the tremendous size of the rooms and by the attention to detail Hearst had specified. In the Assembly Room, the Great Barney Mantel—a French fireplace sixteen feet high—had been in place since 1923; the Palazzo Martinengo ceiling had been there almost as long. These and some of the "built-ins" in the adjoining Main Vestibule were among the first, if not the very first, architectural antiques to be incorporated into the new building. But the choir stalls with which Hearst and Morgan finally chose to unify the widely varied decorative elements in San Simeon's largest room would not be shipped west until 1926, and certain other details in the Assembly Room would not be worked out for a few more years.

*In May of 1926, two oaks were moved in the area near the eventual Theater. Hearst wrote superintendent Camille Rossi, "When you move the big oak trees please do turn them so that the longest branches will extend across the esplanade. This is very important, in fact it is one of the chief reasons for this big work."*

Next door the Refectory awaited an appropriate ceiling. Hearst finally came up with the "Saints" ceiling, which he and Morgan at first thought a compromise, but which was soon regarded as one of San Simeon's premier architectural features. Like the Refectory, the Morning Room and its adjoining Patio Vestibule were only partly complete when the Christmas Eve group sat down to dinner in 1925. Elsewhere on the ground floor, the Service Wing was probably well along in the area that contains the kitchen. But the north side of Casa Grande was quite another matter: beyond the Morning Room, the structure stopped abruptly near a clump of oak trees. There would be no Billiard Room, no Theater, and no Recreation Wing for a few more years.

At the end of 1925 the situation outdoors was largely the same as that inside—some areas looked, or were soon to look, as they do today, whereas others bore little or no resemblance to their eventual form. The Esplanade, one of the major unifying elements in the "harmonious whole" that Hearst had originally projected, had been worked on intermittently since 1923; concrete had finally been poured in April of 1925. The uppermost terraces alongside Casa Grande were also structurally complete. Of these, the two Tea Terraces would be paved and tiled by 1927; the Main Terrace, however, because of extensive changes that included the moving of an oak tree, would not be finished until about 1930. Casa Grande itself showed a raw gray exterior to the Christmas group of 1925. Details like the carved wood cornice for the third floor and the iron window grilles for the Assembly Room were almost ready to go up, but the white Manti stone veneer would not be applied for two more years.

Just below the Esplanade, the small "well terraces" on both sides of the hill were at least structurally complete. One of them would retain its circular shape and would be picturesquely named the North Earring Terrace; the other would be enlarged considerably over the next three years to become simply the South Terrace. Below this intermediate level, a steep, single flight of steps extended down the

*The success of San Simeon's landscape architecture depends on the Esplanade, the curving avenue that encircles Casa Grande and that unites the main building, the three houses, the terraces, and the gardens as the "harmonious whole" envisioned by Hearst in 1919.*

*A proposal for the north end of the Billiard Room, calling for a French Gothic doorway and a Persian tile spandrel under a painted ceiling from Spain. These are precisely the elements that were installed, perhaps soon after this undated drawing was produced.*

The first outdoor swimming pool, completed in time for the summer of 1924, had nearly vanished from the scene before the end of 1925. By then Hearst and Morgan had set their sights on the eventual Neptune Pool, but nearly ten years elapsed before the work was completed. In the meantime, the main pool basin was temporarily enlarged to about three quarters its present size, and at one point a cascade existed where Charles Cassou's Birth of Venus was later installed.

The components of The Birth of Venus wait alongside an intermediate version of the Neptune Pool during the early 1930s. The pool was ultimately widened to the point marked by the small palm tree; the Cassou sculptures mark the eventual site of the north pavilion.

The Birth of Venus, one of several marble groups Hearst commissioned of Charles Cassou for the Neptune Pool, was exhibited at the Salon of 1930 in Paris before it was shipped to San Simeon.

Charles Cassou's monumental Diana group was to have decorated the main entrance, a spot marked by two unfinished flights of stairs between the North Terrace and the driveway. The plan was never carried out, and Diana waited nearby in huge packing crates throughout Hearst's remaining years at San Simeon.

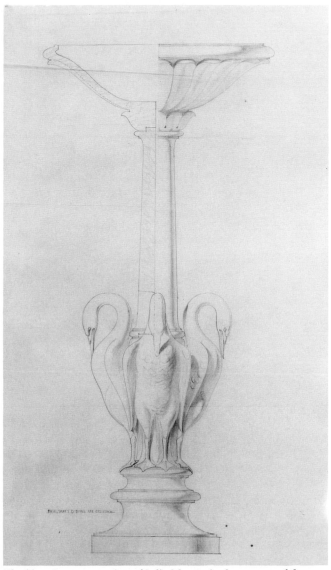

*Thaddeus Joy, an associate of Julia Morgan's, drew many of the ornamental details for San Simeon, often in full scale.*

*One of four sculptured lamp standards by L. Cardini of San Francisco, based on Thaddeus Joy's full-scale drawing. The marble standards are situated on the Neptune Terrace, which overlooks the Neptune Pool.*

north side of the hill, connecting these upper reaches with the driveway. By 1930 the lower half of the long flight would be replaced with a divided staircase and the upper half with the sprawling North Terrace, neither of which features Hearst was ever able to finish.

Outside the core of the "architectural group" are two notable areas that we should also try to visualize—the northwest corner of the hill, where the Neptune Pool lies; and the northeast corner, where the equally magnificent Roman Pool is situated. In 1925 the outdoor pool was a modest basin that gave little indication of the grandeur to come. Three years earlier Hearst had acquired an ancient temple fragment

that soon began to figure in his plans and that would continue to do so for the next twelve years. First, he viewed the temple as an ideal decoration in a proposed garden scheme; next, as a backdrop for a reflecting pond; then, as a focal point for an actual swimming pool. By the summer of 1924 the first version of the swimming pool was ready, but within a year Hearst decided to enlarge it as part of a new plan that would eventually yield a colonnaded pool basin dominated by the centrally placed temple ruin. The stages that led to that design were many and dramatic; not until the mid-1930s would the Neptune Pool assume its present look.

The future site of the Roman Pool boasted nothing more than a tennis

court—a single tennis court, that is— in December of 1925. The following summer Hearst would call for its expansion, but the idea of including an indoor pool probably did not occur to him until later; however, he had been toying with the idea of a saltwater pool. His first thought was to build it near the ocean, but by the summer of 1926 the saltwater pool would join the list of hilltop proposals; by 1927 the proposal would become allied with that for an enlarged tennis court. Construction would begin that year and would continue on and off until 1932, when the Roman Pool, complete with a rooftop pair of tennis courts, would emerge as we see it today. The anticipated use of saltwater had been more than just a whim. As

late as 1931, Julia Morgan's ace engineer, Walter Huber, would be making calculations for a separate saltwater reservoir to adjoin the existing tank on Reservoir Hill. The saltwater was to have been pumped from the ocean to the 1,800-foot summit, from which it would have flowed by gravity to the Roman Pool. The plan was finally abandoned, and the Roman Pool was put on the same freshwater supply line as the rest of the estate.

We should also consider San Simeon's horticulture and landscape architecture. Hearst gave much thought to plants and planting schemes; late in 1920, he arranged the first shipment of nursery stock from Santa Barbara. The hilltop remained devoid of any but native flora, most notably the spreading California live oaks, until this first assortment of trees and shrubs was planted in 1921.

This modest beginning foreshadowed the eventual character of the gardens. Most of the early landscape work was concentrated near the three houses, which, unlike the immense main building, lent themselves to a liberal use of plants in their courtyards and along their exterior walls. (Interestingly enough, the houses were briefly known as Casa Rosa, Casa Bougainvillea, and Casa Heliotrope.) Unquestionably the landscaping of the hilltop had become important by 1925 and would remain so for many years after.

But Hearst thought of far more than garden beds and hedgerows, having cast his eyes on the surrounding, mostly treeless, slopes. In 1922, through George C. Roeding's California Nursery Company in Niles, near San Jose, Hearst and Julia Morgan recruited Nigel Keep, an English "plantsman" of the old school

*Ten years may well have seemed a short wait for results as magnificent as those finally achieved at the Neptune Pool; little wonder visitors today frequently ask whether Hearst and his guests actually swam here. They surely did, and their experience was made all the more exquisite by the heated water Hearst provided.*

who had trained under Roeding, one of the leading nurserymen in the country. Keep, who filled in temporarily as head gardener when he arrived at San Simeon, was hired for a much more ambitious, typically Hearstian task—the development of orchards and the forestation of dozens of acres of barren slopes adjoining La Cuesta Encantada. Keep's best work required many years of growing time for the results to appear. The Christmas group of 1925 probably found little to capture their fancy aside from the landscaping near the buildings. Had they visited San Simeon a decade later, their reactions would have been quite different. By then they would have beheld, among other marvels, the gracefully curving pergola west of the main grounds, a masterpiece of landscape architecture that served both as a bridle path and as a trellis for thousands of fruit trees.

Finally, a quick review of the zoo and the warehouses—two aspects of the estate beyond the hilltop itself, selected from a longer list of possibilities—can round out our visualization of Hearst's principality at the close of 1925.

The zoo was started by 1924, in which year Hearst acquired a herd of forty Montana buffalo. This venture, like many others, would not reach its height for five to ten more years; nevertheless, by Christmas of 1925, enough exotic animals were on hand to astound the guests and thus contribute another dimension to San Simeon's rapidly growing mystique. Along the shorefront, meanwhile, San Simeon village was quite different from what it would become during the next decade. In 1925 there was only one warehouse—the huge "freight shed" built in 1878, a relic from George Hearst's era that still stands across from Sebastian's Store. W. R. Hearst would begin to expand his storage facilities within a year or two, first with a pair of galvanized warehouses (one of which no longer exists), next with a unit resembling a California mission, and finally with another galvanized structure built in the mid-1930s. Only then would the tales of multiple warehouses "bursting at the seams" be true.

*As early as 1919, Hearst spoke of pergolas as possible adjuncts to the proposed buildings. They were never built on the main grounds of the estate, but in 1929 the most ambitious pergola in the annals of California landscape design began to rise on Lone Tree Hill. Soon the "lone tree" was joined by thousands of others planted by orchardist Nigel Keep. The pergola itself was espaliered with fruit trees and grape vines over its entire length of more than a mile.*

*Julia Morgan and one of the beloved members of the San Simeon zoo, Marianne the elephant.*

*No less spectacular than the Neptune Pool, the indoor Roman Pool underwent nearly as many architectural changes, though over a somewhat shorter period of time. The two rooftop tennis courts became the setting for San Simeon's most popular outdoor recreation.*

Nineteen twenty-seven is one of those years that have become ingrained in our national memory. By thinking of events as diverse as Babe Ruth's slugging sixty home runs for the Yankees, Al Jolson's holding millions spellbound with *The Jazz Singer,* and youthful Charles Lindbergh's flying alone across the Atlantic, we can recall a year that epitomizes the prosperous, supremely confident side of the Twenties. The Wall Street crash and the Great Depression lay in wait just around the corner, but in 1927 nothing could have been further from the public's mind. That year also found William Randolph Hearst sixty-four years old and shifting into high gear at San Simeon, as we have seen from the foregoing summary of his and Julia Morgan's progress. Certainly by 1927 —the year in which Hearst first spoke of San Simeon as a museum—the groundwork for the heyday had been solidly laid; and though Hearst's attempts to realize his ever-expanding, ever-changing dream would continue, he could now enjoy the fruits of nearly ten years' work. The heyday had dawned; it would be in full swing within a couple of years and would last until the end of the 1930s.

During these roughly dozen years, from 1927 to about 1940, some of the most colorful guests in San Simeon's social history appeared, beginning, appropriately enough, with Charles Lindbergh, who flew up to the ranch from Los Angeles one weekend while on his nationwide tour in the summer of 1927. (Hearst, a long-time proponent of aviation, had sponsored the historic Dominguez Air Meet in Los Angeles in 1910 and had recently begun flying into San Simeon in a Fokker airplane. He later owned a Stinson and a Vultee, and in the 1940s he built an airstrip large enough for his new DC-3C.) For 1928, the standouts include the swimmer Gertrude Ederle and Jimmy "Beau James" Walker, mayor of New York City. Winston Churchill was easily the most prominent guest in 1929. An airborne visitor in the same year was the *Graf Zeppelin,* whose American tour was sponsored by W. R. Hearst. A Hearst taxi driver noted in his log for August 25 that the famous dirigible passed over San Simeon at 9:37 p.m. and flashed a greeting with its search light; Casa Grande answered by flashing the lights on its twin towers.

Ex-President Calvin Coolidge's week-long stay in the winter of 1930 was one of the highlights that year. According to San Simeon folklore, this was the sole occasion on which Hearst staged a formal dinner, an event that required a special shipment on short notice of evening wear from Los Angeles lest the regulars in the group, accustomed to the prevailing informality, be caught unprepared. The literary world was well represented that same year by the visit of Theodore Dreiser, who lunched with Hearst and pleaded the case of the radical labor leader Tom Mooney.

Perhaps the most memorable guest was the Irish critic and playwright George Bernard Shaw, who arrived in March of 1933 for what was supposedly his only overnight stay in a private residence in this country. Shaw contributed to the Hearst newspapers intermittently for many years, and, though his political views differed greatly from W. R. Hearst's, admired the publisher's individualism and outspokenness. Hearst's feelings toward the acid-tongued Shaw were mutual.

J. Paul Getty's signature appears in the Hearst Castle guest book under the date of January 7, 1935. Toward the end of that year the English literary great H. G. Wells, who had come to Hollywood while his scenario for the futuristic movie *Things to Come* was being filmed, visited Hearst in the company of his good friends Charlie Chaplin and Paulette Goddard. Three years later the sculptor of Mount

*The hub of social life at San Simeon was the ground floor of Casa Grande, where the Assembly Room, Refectory, and Morning Room allowed large groups to gather. All meals were taken at the long tables in the Refectory; Hearst, ever the pivotal figure, always sat in the very center of the room.*

*William Randolph Hearst's April 29th birthday was frequently the occasion for an elaborate costume party. The Marion Davies film* Operator 13, *set in the Deep South during the Civil War, may well have inspired the Confederate theme for one of Hearst's birthday celebrations in the mid-1930s.*

Rushmore, Gutzon Borglum, was at San Simeon; his name appears in the guest book alongside David Niven's.

By far the names that have repeatedly cropped up in accounts of San Simeon are those like Niven's—names of Hollywood directors, actors, scenarists, and others in the film colony who worked on the Marion Davies pictures, the last of which were made in 1937, or who were otherwise acquainted with Miss Davies or Mr. Hearst through the motion picture industry. Too few names, it seems, of the Shaw or Wells or Lindbergh stature are remembered today, primarily because of the attention given the movie colony. Hollywood was important, to be sure; but San Simeon's heyday reflected the much larger social milieu in which W. R. Hearst moved. If additional guest books were to surface (the surviving ones cover only the most limited period), the list of names would probably prove as eye-opening in the realm of social history as the Hearst-Morgan correspondence has proved in that of architecture and construction.

*The garden scheme for La Cuesta Encantada is said to have been inspired by the estate of Hearst's grandmother near San Jose, California. The San Simeon gardens also reflect in part the efforts of Bruce Porter, a San Francisco artist, and Isabella Worn, a prominent horticulturist from the same city. But above all they reflect the combined vision of William Randolph Hearst and Julia Morgan, who gave the gardens as much consideration as they gave every other part of the project.*

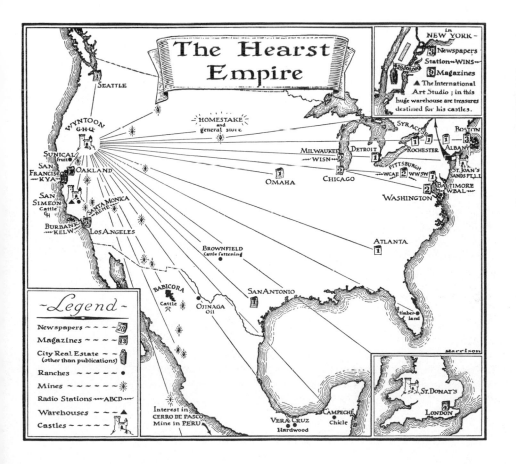

*In 1935,* Fortune *magazine published another feature on Hearst, this time emphasizing the man's business empire. The accompanying map indicated that his northern California estate, Wyntoon, had become his headquarters. In reality, San Simeon and Wyntoon shared that role. By 1935, Hearst's pattern was to use Wyntoon during the summer and San Simeon during the fall, winter, and spring.*

*For sheer magnificence, San Simeon was pre-eminent in Hearst's residential repertoire. But Wyntoon was foremost in conveying a feeling of make-believe, as reflected in the names of the buildings—for example, Angel House, Cinderella House, Brown Bear, and The Gables.*

*True to his statement to Julia Morgan in 1927 that he would "buy only the finest things for the ranch from now on," Hearst acquired this superb pair of Italian maiolica vases through the London art market in 1932.*

*Hearst's lavish European excursions recalled the tradition of the Grand Tour of previous centuries — "Tourism a la Hearst," biographer W. A. Swanberg called them. Hearst spent the summers of 1928, 1930, and 1931 traveling in Europe; his next trip, shown here, took place in 1934, when three of his sons were part of the entourage; he last went abroad in 1936.*

*Hearst and Morgan met the challenge of completing Casa Grande by conceiving a plan for a huge rear wing that would connect the existing wings—but only on paper did they do so. Variously described as an art gallery, a tapestry wing, a banqueting hall, a grand ballroom—or even as a combination of these things—the proposed wing became increasingly infeasible as the Depression continued. Construction at San Simeon ceased altogether by the late 1930s, and though work resumed in 1945 and continued for two more years, the great wing was never begun.*

William Randolph Hearst turned seventy on April 29, 1933. A large crowd gathered at San Simeon and presented the Chief, as Hearst was called by his employees, with a thick volume filled with tributes from his top newspapermen and executives. But this was no retirement party. despite the retrospective gesture. The Hearst newspaper chain had become a colossus since World War I, expanding from a dozen metropolitan dailies in 1919 to more than twice that number in the 1930s. Hearst had also multiplied his holdings in radio, motion pictures and newsreels, magazines, and news and feature services. An elaborate organizational network kept the great empire running, but Hearst himself remained the supreme commander, the mastermind—the Chief. He also

remained the Lord of San Simeon. By glancing at the estate, one could see that Hearst had influenced the project at every turn; one could also see that the man still had plenty of work ahead of him. "The time to retire is when God retires you, and not before," said William Randolph Hearst. Retirement in that form would not claim him for eighteen more years.

But the road had become rough by 1933. The Depression had hit bottom, and Hearst was in a quandary over the prospect of finishing San Simeon. Could he continue the project, even on the reduced basis he and Julia Morgan had adopted? Some of the papers were running alarmingly in the red as the national crisis deepened; the capital required to revitalize them might leave too little for San Simeon—or for Wyntoon, the Tyrolean summer retreat Hearst had begun developing in northern California. If the construction crew

were cut back further, some of the big jobs, like the Neptune Pool or Hearst's own Gothic Study, might drag on unduly; certain proposals, most notably the connecting back wing for Casa Grande, might not get past the drawing board. (The former were completed during the next two years; the latter was never begun.) One of the misconceptions about Hearst is that he never intended to finish San Simeon, that he would have built and re-built and tinkered and altered indefinitely, with no particular regard for the outcome. True, Hearst had consistently followed his own axiom: "There is always time to make a thing better." But now time was beginning to run out. Hearst owed it to Julia Morgan, to his family and his friends, and, above all, to himself and his future place in history to complete San Simeon if he could, to make it the "harmonious whole" he had spoken of years earlier.

But he was not about to let his deeper concerns interfere with the enjoyment of the moment. San Simeon still offered the most enviable social experience of the era, not only for the Hollywood crowd, but also for an unlimited array of notable people. The heyday flourished despite the Depression and the near break-up of the Hearst empire in 1937. W. R. Hearst coolly maintained his regal bearing during these precarious, trying times; with the aplomb befitting this most accomplished of hosts, he continued to enthrall his guests until the debacle of Pearl Harbor prompted him to close San Simeon and reside in the mountain fastness of Wyntoon. But an observant guest during the late 1930s would have noticed that, for all the buoyancy and gaiety, something was quite different.

*Hearst's last active year of art collecting before the Second World War was 1937. It was then that he acquired Franz-Xaver Winterhalter's portraits of Emperor Maximilian and Empress Charlotte, painted in Paris in 1864. The portraits were hung in Casa del Mar, Hearst's original house and the one that he returned to when he came back to San Simeon in 1944. He resumed active collecting that same year and continued the pursuit until his death in 1951.*

The noise and bustle of construction, so dear to William Randolph Hearst, had fallen uncommonly silent.

San Simeon reopened late in 1944. Hearst was now nearly eighty-two, but his dream of building still burned within him. In the fall of 1945 a big crew resumed work for the first time in nearly a decade, enlarging the wings of Casa Grande, especially the New Wing, as the northern one was now called. The revival lasted until May of 1947, when poor health forced Mr. Hearst to bid San Simeon farewell. Four years later, he died in Beverly Hills. He was buried alongside his parents at Cypress Lawn cemetary near San Francisco, the city of his birth.

The journey from San Francisco in 1863, to New York in 1895, back to California thirty years later, and finally back to his birthplace in 1951 was an eighty-eight-year odyssey for William Randolph Hearst. It was one of the most remarkable odysseys in American history—all the more so for Hearst's having created that jewel of the California coast, La Cuesta Encantada.

*The Neptune Pool required one last detail to be truly complete—the installation of Charles Cassou's* Neptune *group in the alcove behind the same artist's* Birth of Venus (above). *Cassou completed the dramatic sculpture in his Paris studio in the late Thirties (see plaster mock-up, below); but, with building at a standstill by then,* Neptune *never got any closer to San Simeon than Hearst's warehouse in New York.*

*Nineteen Forty-seven was William Randolph Hearst's last year at San Simeon. The staff was alerted on more than one occasion that Mr. Hearst would soon be returning from Beverly Hills, but the aged publisher, though mentally keen and still in control of his great empire, never saw La Cuesta Encantada again.*

# THE LEGACY:
## HEARST SAN SIMEON STATE HISTORICAL MONUMENT

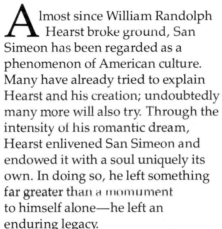

Almost since William Randolph Hearst broke ground, San Simeon has been regarded as a phenomenon of American culture. Many have already tried to explain Hearst and his creation; undoubtedly many more will also try. Through the intensity of his romantic dream, Hearst enlivened San Simeon and endowed it with a soul uniquely its own. In doing so, he left something far greater than a monument to himself alone—he left an enduring legacy.

Millions have seen San Simeon since 1958, thanks to the Hearst Corporation, whose gift of La Cuesta Encantada to the California State Parks System opened the way to public access. Millions more will be able to see San Simeon, thanks to the State itself, whose ongoing maintenance and conservation efforts have ensured that the legacy of William Randolph Hearst will be preserved.

The following overview of La Cuesta Encantada emphasizes the art collection Hearst assembled during a fifty-year period but includes something of the architecture, the landscaping, and the other features of Hearst San Simeon State Historical Monument as well.

### THE HOUSES

*Casa del Mar* (House "A"). The largest house commands a superlative view of the Hearst Ranch and San Simeon Bay. This was Mr. Hearst's own house until he moved into Casa Grande in the late 1920s, but he remained fond of Casa del Mar and reoccupied his old suite during his final years at San Simeon. The building is more richly decorated than the two other houses and even more so than much of Casa Grande. The twentieth century "built-in" collection is stunningly represented by gilded and polychromed plaster of Paris window trims and ceilings—the products of craftsmen who supplied a great number of works either copied from antique originals or based on new designs by Julia Morgan and her staff. Mostly Italian motifs were selected for the upper floor; Mrs. Hearst's original suite, for example, contains a ceiling copied by Theo Van der Loo from the Church of Santa Maria in Aracoeli, Rome. Among the fine arts here, three paintings are particularly interesting. The first is Adriaen Ysenbrandt's *Madonna and Child with Two Angels,* considered by some to be San Simeon's finest painting; the two others are portraits by Franz-Xaver

*Probably no furnishing or art object at San Simeon is more famous than the Cardinal Richelieu Bed, an Italian Baroque piece in Casa del Monte. Former guests have mentioned the bed in their memoirs, and many travel writers have made almost awed reference to it. Only recently has it come to light that the "Cardinal Richelieu" story stemmed purely from the imagination of Camille Rossi, the construction superintendent from 1922 to 1932.*

*Casa Grande, or the "Castle," resembles a cathedral, primarily because of its twin towers, which were inspired by Santa Maria la Mayor in Ronda, Spain. The most striking feature on the facade is the dark wooden gable on Hearst's private third floor, a 1920s production in Siamese teak by Jules Suppo. The ground floor consists of large social rooms whereas the upper floors, except for Hearst's level, consist mostly of guests suites.*

*Akin to the great Magnolia Vase made by Tiffany & Co. for exhibition at the World's Columbian Exposition in Chicago in 1893, Phoebe Apperson Hearst's enameled silver vase-lamp was made by the same company and represents Victorian opulence at its height. (Assembly Room)*

Winterhalter of the ill-fated Emperor Maximilian and Empress Charlotte of Mexico.

The contemporary plasterwork in the lower suite shows a Spanish influence. Among the furnishings are two huge bedsteads, one of which is completely gilded and comes from the Davanzati Palace in Florence. In the same bedroom hangs a portrait of Archduke Ferdinand of Austria at age fifteen, the work of Christoph Amberger, a German master. In the central lobby is a marble table inlaid with semiprecious stones in the design of the Medici family crest; nearby is a polychrome stucco relief by Mino da Fiesole or a related sculptor of the 1400s. A Roman theme distinguishes the adjoining loggia, where a mosaic from North Africa, a massive stone table, a child's sarcophagus, and a large garden bust are the principal decorations.

***Casa del Monte*** (House "B"). The smallest house faces Junipero Serra Peak, the highest summit in the Santa Lucia Range. The exterior of the building is deceptively plain, with its broad expanses of white stucco; but the elaborate cast stone ornamentation hints at the richness of the interior, which recalls a sumptuous Renaissance villa. For the main sitting room a graystone mantel, a Venetian giltwood doorway, and a crimson red valance establish an Italianate mood. Pairs of French and Italian cabinets line the side walls; between the latter two is an armorial *cassone*—a low, elongated chest—of the Barberini family.

A mountain-view room contains the Cardinal Richelieu Bed, actually an Italian Baroque production so named by Camille Rossi, Julia Morgan's flamboyant construction superintendent through most of the 1920s. No bed could have been more deserving of Rossi's whimsy: the solid-slab sides and the elaborately carved headboard, which displays the arms of the Boffa family of Lombardy, are extremely unusual. In the same room is a gentleman's portrait by a sixteenth-century German master. Elsewhere in the building are giltwood saints and angels; a superb gold-embroidered cope; an early

English alabaster of the Virgin, saints, and surrounding angels; and Chinese hardstone sculptures fitted as lamps.

*Casa del Sol* (House "C"). Middle in location and in size of the outlying trio, Casa del Sol looks west toward Point Piedras Blancas, whose lighthouse dates from 1874. The Moorish style of plasterwork and the related architectural decoration of the 1920s convey an Oriental flavor that combines agreeably with the prevalent Spanish and Italian influences at San Simeon; many of the furnishings exhibit Mohammedan overtones as well. The building contains, among other works, inlaid and gilded *varguenos,* which are drop-front desks; carved walnut tables; statuettes of saints; provincial paintings of religious subjects; and, in the main sitting room, full-length portraits by Bartolome Gonzales of a young prince and his sister. Intricately hammered silver lamps add a note of luxury and richness.

Italian furnishings fill in alongside, and Persian objects are also present. These range from iridescent blue Sultanabad vases—some of which are 800 years old—to turn-of-the-century rugs and carpets. The finest are woven of silk or very high-grade wool and are used as wall hangings in the larger bedrooms.

A Baroque portal decorates the opening from the Main Vestibule into the Assembly Room. The giltwood columns are Spanish architectural fragments from the Hearst Collection; the matching overdoor section is 1920s plaster of Paris work by Theo Van der Loo. To either side can be seen some of the choir stalls that line the room; above them hang two of four "Scipio" tapestries from the sixteenth century.

The end alcoves of the Assembly Room are themselves virtually great halls. Concealed from view on the far right is the elevator Hearst used each evening to come from his private suite down to this level, where he joined his guests before dinner.

The pristine whiteness of the **Venus** of Canova is accentuated by a dark backdrop of Italian Renaissance choir stalls. *(Assembly Room)*

## CASA GRANDE (The Main Building)

The "Castle" is a honeycomb of roughly 100 rooms—a "three-dimensional jigsaw puzzle," as a keen observer has called it. The physical complexity of Casa Grande is equalled, if not outdone, by its stylistic complexity and uniqueness. Many are the wealthy who have built great palaces and country houses, but how many have virtually created their own cathedral? This and related questions that come to mind are too intricate, too baffling to address here. Suffice it to say that the main building embodies Hearst's romantic vision as thoroughly as anything that the man could have produced. Improbable and unconventional an architectural statement as Casa Grande may be, one can hardly imagine anything more impressive or more astounding —or more beautiful.

*Assembly Room* (first floor). Here are found some of the most imposing items in the Hearst Collection as well as some of the finest. In the adjoining vestibule a sculptured marble doorway bearing the arms of Pope Julius II can be seen; a Roman mosaic floor identified as "Merman and Fishes" paves the same entryway. In the Assembly Room itself an immense carved wood ceiling is displayed. Neptune appears in one coffered section, Jupiter in another; the central coffer displays the crest of the Martinengo family of Brescia, Italy. The Great Barney Mantel—named for Charles T. Barney, a previous owner— stands against the east wall; choir stalls from Italian Renaissance churches flank the huge fireplace and also line the opposite wall. Together with the ceiling, the mantel, a large gilded doorway, and a superb display of Flemish tapestries, the choir-stall paneling provides a regal backdrop.

*Literally a Renaissance jewel, this French presentation casket of rock crystal, ebony, gilt bronze, and semiprecious stones dates from the 1500s and, despite its relatively small size, is the focal point in San Simeon's largest room.*

The tapestries deserve top billing. Hearst acquired many important single panels, pairs, and partial and complete sets during his long years of collecting. The Assembly Room contains four panels from a ten-piece set of "Scipio" tapestries that were woven in Brussels in the sixteenth century; they portray the deeds of Scipio Africanus, the Roman general who defeated Hannibal during the Second Punic War. Tapestries of a later but equally important vintage hang above the windows; one of them is the *Triumph of the Church,* based on a design by Peter Paul Rubens.

Marbles and other sculptures are also noteworthy. Circular reliefs by the neoclassicist Bertel Thorvaldsen are displayed in the upper reaches of the end walls. The same sculptor's *Venus Triumphant* stands in one corner, and in another is the *Venus of Canova,* which Antonio Canova carved, and which Lucien Bonaparte once owned.

Smaller treasures range from a Tiffany & Co. silver vase-lamp, formerly Phoebe Hearst's, to a remarkable jewel, or presentation, casket. Made primarily of rock crystal and dating from the sixteenth century, the casket was a gift from French & Company in 1927, a major art-dealing firm with which Hearst did a lively trade.

*Jean Leon Gerome's* Pygmalion and Galatea *entered the Hearst Collection in 1910. Originally considered as a decoration for Casa del Mar, the marble sculpture was placed instead in the Main Vestibule, the entryway that adjoins the Assembly Room.*

*Refectory* (first floor). Art of the late Middle Ages prevails: saints and madonnas set the religious mood, which is both solemn and romantic. Four centuries is an average age for many of San Simeon's art works, but here their ages are apt to be greater; at the end of the room the gilt-iron Spanish *reja,* a screen from a cathedral, is more than 600 years old. Other "built-ins" include portions of a French cloister, an enormous Gothic mantelpiece, the "Saints" ceiling from Italy, and a set of Spanish choir stalls from the early 1400s.

The silver, however, is the show-stopper here—candlesticks, serving dishes, a large wine cistern, a parliamentary mace, and a bishop's processional banner. Hearst was a renowned collector of silver; in all his other homes a fair share was displayed or kept in storage for special occasions, and San Simeon was no exception. Most of the silver in the Refectory dates from the eighteenth century. The exceptions are the bishop's banner, which is 300 years old, and the mace and a Sheffield warming dish, both of which date from the nineteenth century.

The four matching tables come from an Italian convent. When Hearst acquired them in the 1920s, they were said to form the finest set of its kind in this country. A fifth, non-matching table comes from England. But the origin of the twenty-two X-frame "Dante" chairs remains unknown. A small number are evidently antique originals; the rest are expertly made copies produced either in New York or in Europe for San Simeon.

In the tapestry category are two Flemish Gothic panels and a later weaving from the Baroque period. The former depict the prophet Daniel's encounter with the great Babylonian king Nebuchadnezzar II. The other tapestry, an heirloom from the Phoebe Hearst Collection, is entitled *The Encounter.* This high-spirited work adds a welcome burst of color to the east end of the Refectory, much as the twenty-four banners add a cheerful note to the main walls of the room.

**Morning Room** (first floor). The Gothic, medieval character is maintained with a heavily timbered ceiling, a cathedral archway of marble, a chateau mantlepiece, and doors that bear the IHS insignia—the sacred monogram of Christ. A contrasting classical note is found in the adjoining Patio Vestibule, where a Roman mosaic and two ancient torsos are displayed.

Sanctuary lamps of silver hang from the ceiling in the Morning Room. The decorations on these lamps, like the decorations on much of the silver at San Simeon, are examples of repousse, a technique of hammering highly detailed designs from the back side of the thin, rolled-out sheets of silver. Hearst's electrification of the lamps typifies the modernizing of antique fixtures that was popular during his era.

The four tapestries here come from a seventeenth-century workshop; their pastoral scenes provide a charming and restful departure from the historical, religious, and allegorical subjects in other rooms.

*The Morning Room, or Breakfast Room as it is also called, runs perpendicular to the Refectory at the back of Casa Grande. The medieval theme is strongly carried out by the red marble arch on the left and by the wood ceiling, both of which are Spanish, and by the stone mantelpiece from a French chateau. The hanging lamps of hammered silver are from Italy and Spain.*

Compared with the garishness of most American movie palaces of the 1930s, the Theater at San Simeon is a model of dignity and restraint. Hearst enjoyed watching a movie after a long day of managing his myriad business affairs; he and Marion Davies sat in the front row, and the remaining forty-eight chairs were sufficient for all but the very largest groups of guests.

Hearst's love of the Middle Ages attained its fullest expression in his own Gothic Suite, which few guests ever saw, and in the Refectory, which was open to all. Silver gleams against a somewhat severe but sumptuous backdrop that includes a French Gothic mantelpiece, a Flemish tapestry from the "Daniel" set, and carved wood choir stalls from Seo de Urgel, a cathedral in northern Spain. The central arrangement of two long tables and twenty-two chairs was sufficient for most occasions, but a third or even fourth table could easily be added to accommodate larger groups.

*A constant delight to the eye but a riddle to the art historians who have studied it, the Billiard Room's hunting tapestry is, in all likelihood, one of a pair. The companion tapestry, which was last accounted for in another American collection, has been of unknown whereabouts for many years, making the Hearst panel a great rarity.*

**Billiard Room** (first floor). From the Spanish ceiling of the 1400s and the French mantel and doorways of the same period, the medieval scene shifts to Persia, with brilliantly glazed tile pictures from the ancient city of Ispahan. The two oldest panels consist of forty-eight tiles each and date from the sixteenth century. The largest tile picture is an arched spandrel of 100 pieces that tells the story of Joseph and Potiphar's wife; the two smallest panels have twenty-four tiles apiece.

The focal point of the room is a Gothic tapestry simply entitled *Hunting Scene.* This *millefleur* 'thousand flower' weaving is one of San Simeon's most delightful works and an ideal choice for the Billiard Room. The tapestry compliments the paintings of sporting activities on the old ceiling, the dragon hunt and the entertainment scenes in the Persian tiles, and even the pool and billiard tables. The more delicate side of the collection is found here too; the foremost example is a French jewel cabinet dated 1562.

**Theater** (first floor). A small panel of tiles similar to those in the Billiard Room decorates the entry hall to the Theater. Below the panel stands an old choir stall that houses the carillon keyboard, from which Casa Grande's thirty-six bells are still played occasionally. The Theater itself contains some richly gilded plasterwork; seventeenth-century Italian damask covers the long side walls.

*The play of light and shadow accentuates the vigorous forms in a Venetian Gothic loggia, the most prominent architectural feature of the Doge's Suite.*

*A rare Italian maiolica inkstand of the sixteenth century, depicting St. George and the dragon. The hole in St. George's upraised right hand is designed to hold a writing implement—and to provide the horseman with a dragon-slaying spear (Doge's Sitting Room).*

*Doge's Suite* (mezzanine level). Hearst's California equivalent of the Doge's Palace in Venice is San Simeon's largest guest suite. The painted ceilings are Italian, except for one rare Dutch example; two of the carved mantelpieces are also Italian, as are the marble arches in the sitting room and, facing the back patio, the Venetian Gothic balcony that gave the suite its name. The other architectural features are mostly Spanish—gilt-iron grilles in the vestibules, sacristy and palace doors, and two Baroque altar columns that were copied to make a twelve-piece set for the suite.

The display of Italian walnut furniture includes several pieces whose craftmanship and velvety patina are of the highest quality. Many examples have drawer fronts veneered with root walnut; one pair of tables has slab tops of multicolored marble. The paintings are predominantly Italian, as are a variety of decorative arts that include a maiolica inkstand of St. George and the dragon, a needlework table cover, and a stucco relief in the style of the Florentine master Agostino di Duccio.

Treasures from other lands include German silver sconces, decorative glass by Rene Lalique, an embroidered altar frontal from the Phoebe Hearst Collection, and Chinese hardstone sculpture lamps.

*The metalwork collection is distinguished by many examples of master craftsmanship, such as these Venetian bronze andirons in the South Doge's Bedroom.*

*Originally known as the Royal Suite, the mezzanine space between the Morning Room and the Cloisters was renamed the Doge's Suite by the time the sitting room and flanking bedrooms were first used in the mid-1920s. Here are found numerous art objects and furnishings of the highest quality the San Simeon collection has to offer.*

In 1927, Hearst spoke of the "superior warmth and comfort" of the Library, a quality that this quietly grand room has always conveyed.
F. M. Lorenz and Jules Suppo carved the walnut bookcases in San Francisco; the design was inspired by an Italian original Hearst acquired in 1921.
The honeycombed ceiling comes from a castle in Aragon and is one of many Spanish examples at San Simeon. Part of Hearst's renowned collection
of Greek pottery can be seen on the plate rail above the bookcases.

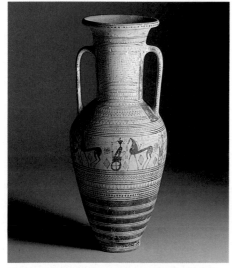

Known as the Baring amphora because of its
previous owner, the English collector Cecil
Baring, this example of the Geometric period
in Greek pottery dates from the eighth century
B.C. and is the oldest specimen in the Library.
A painted frieze of charioteers decorates the
tall-necked amphora.

Nineteeth-century gilt bronze group representing Minerva by Emmanuel Fremiet, a Frenchman
who excelled in his sculptures of animal subjects (Library).

*Library* (second floor). This spacious room is one of the largest at San Simeon and also one of the most restful and serene. Three ceiling sections from Aragon, Spain—evidently from separate rooms in the same building—were combined here as a single unit. Six matching Spanish lanterns, one of the most attractive sets in the collection, hang from the sixteenth-century ceiling. San Simeon's largest Italian mantel stands opposite the picture window; on both sides of the fireplace and around the rest of the room are bookcases carved in the Italian Renaissance style during the 1920s. Their shelves are well stocked with mostly nineteenth- and twentieth-century books.

The room contains the usual Western European furnishings, but the foremost objects are Greek vases and related antiquities. Hearst followed the largely London-based Greek pottery market for fifty years—from 1901 until his death in 1951. He once owned more than 400 vases, of which roughly one third have remained at San Simeon. They range from 2,200 to 2,700 years of age and exemplify most of the major types, such as Athenian, Corinthian, Etruscan, and South Italian. The styles also range widely: some are painted, or "figured," pieces; others are monochromatic, or undecorated. On a related classical note are Roman busts, a Roman marble vase, and an Etruscan bronze *cista,* a type of toiletries container.

### *The Cloisters and Adjoining Rooms*

(second floor). The style of the four Cloister guest rooms is distinctly Spanish-Moorish. Each of the rooms contains an unpainted, rustically carved wood ceiling. In the westernmost Cloister is an unusual English Gothic mantel whose alabaster breastwork displays carved figures of saints. Spanish and Italian furniture and decorative works are freely combined throughout these rooms, and objects as diverse as Chinese pewter jars, a Tiffany Studios inkwell, and Della Robbia glazed reliefs are also present. The easternmost member of the quartet, in fact, bears the variant name of Della Robbia Room.

*Glazed terra cotta relief bearing the arms of Giovanni Maria del Monte—later Pope Julius III—by the Florentine sculptor Giovanni della Robbia. The wreath border includes not only the characteristic fruits and leaves, which are especially crisp in this example, but also two snails (Della Robbia Room).*

The two Deck Rooms, which flank the Della Robbia Room, resemble the Cloisters both architecturally and decoratively. The larger Duplex suites, however, are more akin to the Renaissance and Baroque style of the Assembly Room, although on a far smaller scale befitting their status as guest accommodations. Spiral staircases and boldly protruding bedroom lofts make the four Duplexes some of the most spatially complex, visually fascinating rooms at San Simeon.

*One of four Duplexes, a series of guest suites at the back of Casa Grande. Each of these somewhat narrow, elongated rooms consists of a bath tucked underneath a bedroom at one end and, in the main part of the suite, a sitting area that is open to the high ceiling.*

*Gothic Suite* (third floor). Here we encounter the inner side of William Hearst. The Gothic Suite was Hearst's private domain, and thus we step into a personal realm—not necessarily grander or more ornate than the other parts of the building, but more medieval, more church-like and monastic. Old ceilings are found in each room (except in the Gothic Lobby, which has a remarkable plaster ceiling of the 1920s); and wherever Hearst could incorporate antique doors, doorways, or mantelpieces, he did. The common denominator here is not a national style, such as Spanish or Italian or French, but an overall medieval, Gothic feeling. Thus a fourteenth-century Aragonese ceiling in the south bedroom and a roughhewn, possibly English ceiling in the nearby sitting room are perfectly at home together. Appropriately, the paintings, sculptures, furniture, and decorative arts throughout the third floor are predominantly medieval.

The Gothic Study, which adjoins the bedroom suite and runs at right angles to the back end of Casa Grande, reflects the same medieval tendencies but even more richly and extensively, with accents of silver gilt, bronze, ivory, and brass. Guild cups, plates, tankards, small candlesticks, church pieces, and some purely ornamental objects demonstrate the incredible skill and painstaking craftsmanship of medieval and Renaissance masters of their trades. Most of these pieces are displayed in the recessed niches below the shelf sections of the carved and inlaid bookcases, which were produced in the 1930s; the books themselves are comparable to those in the second-floor Library. At the far end of the room is a painting that no visitor should miss, a portrait of William Randolph Hearst as a young man painted in 1894 by Orrin Peck, Hearst's close friend.

*The North Gothic Bedroom is a gallery of fourteenth- and fifteenth-century Italian paintings, one of which depicts the madonna and child surrounded by saints.*

[1]*Among the precious objects displayed in Hearst's Gothic Study is a buffalo horn whose gilt copper mounting terminates in the claws of a griffin —hence the name "griffinclaw" for this German curio of the 1400s.*

*San Simeon's oldest painting dates from the early 1300s and is attributed to Duccio de Buoninsegna or his follower Segna di Buonaventura. The small panel was a gift from Hearst's close friend and publishing associate Eleanor Patterson of Washington, D.C. (South Gothic Bedroom).*

[1]*Many visitors are surprised by the modest size of William Randolph Hearst's bedroom; perhaps many expect the largest, most dazzling room in Casa Grande. But the showman in Hearst virtually disappeared within the private world of his Gothic Suite. Here the contemplative, somewhat brooding side of Hearst —the medievalist side —held sway.*

*San Hipolito, a Spanish polychromed wood group, is one of several sculptures in the East Room, a secluded alcove adjoining the Gothic Study that few have had a chance to see, in either Hearst's era or today.*

*Celestial Suite* (fourth floor). The impact of the tower suite comes more from the contemporary architectural details than from the collection itself, but the relatively small rooms allow close viewing of some choice works. A glazed terra cotta statue of St. Anthony by Andrea della Robbia is the highlight of the south bedroom; the north bedroom contains an equally interesting carved wood figure of St. John the Baptist from Spain. In the central sitting room four paintings, three of which are nineteenth-century French, deserve attention. Luc Olivier-Merson's *Rest on the Flight into Egypt,* which was exhibited at the Paris Salon of 1879, hangs above the mantel; nearby are two canvases depicting Napoleon Bonaparte, a favorite historical subject of Hearst's, painted by Jean Leon Gerome. One shows Bonaparte overlooking Cairo; the other, *Bonaparte in Egypt,* shows the general seated on horseback before the Sphinx. The fourth painting, a fifteenth-century altarpiece by Giovanni di Piero da Pisa, decorates the back side of the freestanding fireplace structure. The mantel itself is an ingenious blend of a Romanesque limestone frame, eight Spanish picture tiles, and cast stone work from the San Simeon mold shops.

*Billiard Room Wing.* The three guest bedrooms stacked one above the other over the first-floor Billiard Room connect the larger New Wing to the central shank of Casa Grande. These were the last rooms finished in the main building before World War II. All three have a medieval, heavily rusticated quality reminiscent of the Gothic Suite.

*The three bedrooms that lie between the North Duplexes and the New Wing form the upper part of the Billiard Room Wing, which was named for the underlying Billiard Room. The uppermost bedroom speaks well for all three, with its decorative wood ceiling and window frames—the work of F. M. Lorenz of San Francisco—and its English Gothic bed of the Henry VII period.*

*A narrow porch known as the Celestial Bridge provides access to both bell towers from the fourth-floor Celestial Suite. The panorama from this level is one of the most spectacular at San Simeon; the Bridge also affords an ideal view of the tile decoration that is concentrated in these highest parts of Casa Grande.*

*The influence of Art Deco became apparent at San Simeon during the 1920s and '30s, but not until the late 1940s did Art Deco truly come into its own at La Cuesta Encantada, as epitomized by this marble-lined bath on the second floor of the New Wing.*

*Many of San Simeon's paintings hang in the New Wing. In the west bedroom of the third floor, for example, is this portrait of a noblewoman, a work attributed to the Italian master Giulio Campi. As Burton Fredericksen of the J. Paul Getty Museum has aptly written, "It is an exceptionally forceful portrait, and an unforgettable image."*

**The New Wing.** A pronounced Spanish theme, often with Moorish overtones, characterizes the entire New Wing, the three-level section above the Theater on the north side of Casa Grande. Antique ceilings, doors, and lanterns from various parts of Spain are abundant enough to constitute a major gallery of architectural elements. Plain white walls give the rooms a contemporary feeling and allow greater visibility of paintings,

hanging rugs, and other decorative works than do many other parts of the estate. And as for modern, domestic details, the marble-lined baths throughout this 1940s section are nothing less than spectacular. The second floor contains about 3,000 square feet, generously divided among a pair of three-room suites and a spacious entry hall; the same is true of the third floor. The top floor is slightly smaller but even more impressive than the lower floors because of the higher ceilings in its tower suites.

The architectural collection on the second floor includes three very attractive ceilings. The west bedroom contains an intricately carved example from the sixteenth century; the adjoining sitting room contains one a

century older from the Castillo de la Luna in Segovia; and the rear suite houses an unusual tile-and-beam combination from Seville. The decorative arts are abundant and varied here. Three examples in the larger sitting room can speak for the entire second floor: the two Peruvian tapestries that were woven for a Spanish viceroy, the eight-legged Portuguese table, and the powder-blue Chinese vase that was made into an electric lamp. The display of paintings includes, in the west bedroom, a small portrait said to be of William Shakespeare; and, in the rear suite, one of San Simeon's premier works, the *Virgin of the Pillar* by Claudio Coello. This depicts a little-known story in which the Virgin Mary tells St. James to erect a shrine on the spot marked by a large column.

On the third floor the architectural elements are equally impressive; the foremost example is the fifteenth-century convent ceiling in the larger sitting room. A matching set of Italian needlepointed furniture in the same room speaks well for the decorative arts on this floor, as does Fanny Rozet's *Cupid Jailed*, an Art Deco night-light in the adjoining bedroom; another memorable piece is the Portuguese canopied bedstead in the rear suite. One of the most stunning pictures in the Hearst Collection hangs in the west bedroom —*Portrait of a Lady,* attributed to Giulio Campi. Next door is a matching pair of Flemish portraits said to represent a seventeen-year-old woman, Aysma van Lauta, and a forty-year-old man, Ripperda, both of whom are elaborately dressed. The rear suite also contains some good paintings, especially the madonna-and-child *tondo*, a round panel, attributed to Cristoforo Caselli.

The top floor is said to have been earmarked for William Randolph Hearst's eventual use. but these and other rooms in the New Wing were not ready for occupancy when Hearst left San Simeon in 1947. Not surprisingly, there is a greater emphasis here on medieval and religious works. The West Tower suite contains a magnificient domed ceiling from Salamanca, part of a set of marble columns from Granada, and,

*Between the lower suites on the top floor of the New Wing lies the Center Room, a smaller equivalent in many ways of the Gothic Study in the central part of Casa Grande. The similarity may well have stemmed from Hearst's intention to occupy these rooms, which many consider the most attractive of those finished in the 1940s.*

in contrast, a French Gothic mantelpiece. Examples of silver, always a Hearst favorite, are displayed here—a richly decorated tabernacle above the fireplace and a door panel now used as a wall hanging. A Spanish armorial carpet and a Persian inscription carpet of fine silk are also used as wall hangings. The adjoining Center Room is a fantasyland of fairy-tale murals painted by Camille Solon, and the East Tower suite at the back of the floor is an architectural complement to the West Tower. Here are found more of the marble columns from Granada, a domed ceiling from the same city, and another French fireplace. Next to the fireplace is a precious, velvet-mounted triptych from Italy, and above the Florentine bed hangs a luxurious Kashan silk carpet.

**The Service Wing.** The smaller counterpart of the New Wing provided housing for the domestic staff, which consisted of roughly twenty people during San Simeon's peak years. The ground-floor Kitchen and Pantry are practical, institutional rooms—a Julia Morgan trademark. The handsome monel serving tables in the Pantry are virtual museum specimens, however, and the display of china, silverware, and glassware is impressive.

*Wine Cellar and Bowling Alley.* Beneath the north end of the Assembly Room lies an area that is as plain architecturally as it was when the forms were stripped from its concrete walls in the 1920s, but the subterranean cool of this basement space proved ideal as a wine cellar. Nearly 5,000 bottles remained in the mid-1950s; undoubtedly the stock was even more extensive during the heyday. The wines and spirits displayed today are both imported and domestic. Some bottles date from the nineteenth century.

The Bowling Alley, as the unfinished area beneath the Theater and New Wing is called, has been put to good use by the State as a conservation room and "museum basement." Though Hearst never installed the lanes and equipment he proposed in the 1930s, the space has been known as the Bowling Alley ever since.

*Leopoldo Ansiglioni's sculpture of a Greek water nymph is the highlight of the Main Terrace. Dating from the 1880s,* Galatea *was carved in Rome by Ansiglioni about the same time he produced a portrait bust of a real-life subject, the youthful William Randolph Hearst.*

*Copy in Carrara marble of* The Wrestlers, *one of two such works by the Romanelli Brothers that flank the steps leading from the Esplanade to the courtyard of Casa del Monte.*

## GROUNDS AND POOLS

***Upper Terraces and Esplanade Area.***
On the Main Terrace—the city square of La Cuesta Encantada—is Leopoldo Ansiglioni's *Galatea,* a highly romantic work that establishes a lighthearted, even playful mood for the younger garden sculptures. The majority of the works outdoors, however, are comparable in age and historical stature to the interior collection; in fact, the oldest works of all—four Egyptian sculptures of the goddess Sekhmet—are only a few steps from Galatea's fishpond. Two large Southern magnolias, a deodar cedar, a native California live oak, and a thick hedge of pink azaleas shield the Main Terrace from the outlying grounds, thus creating an intimate, secluded cove at the foot of Casa Grande. This integration of architecture, landscaping, and art objects characterizes the principal garden areas and terraces. It is one of San Simeon's most memorable attributes.

The adjoining Tea Terraces are decorated with objects ranging from Renaissance wellheads to Roman sarcophagi—ancient coffins carved from sold stone or marble blocks. A level below lies the Esplanade, along whose landscaped avenue statuary, architectural fragments, and sculptured pieces abound. One can have the best glimpse of the Esplanade by starting at the northerly section known as "azalea walk," proceeding past the three houses, and continuing around to the other side of the hill.

A massive lidded sarcophagus flanked by four Italian columns is the first decorative grouping encountered; the columns once formed part of a cloister but are here used as freestanding pedestals, ideal for the display of garden busts. Near Casa del Monte, the roses assume a center-stage role—bush roses, tree roses, and climbing varieties that have latched onto the evenly spaced Mexican fan palms. Across from Casa del Monte stands another Roman sarcophagus; the nine Muses and figures of Apollo and Athena are portrayed on its narrow,

*Detail of the "Muses" sarcophagus, showing Thalia holding a comic mask and Melpomene holding the club of Hercules.*

*Renaissance columns and a bower of roses frame San Simeon's premier example of classical art, a third-century Roman sarcophagus that is decorated with figures representing Apollo and Athena and the nine Muses.*

*The South Terrace and Casa del Mar from a vantage point along the Esplanade near the front of Casa Grande.*

*Opposite Casa del Mar stands* The Three Graces, *a copy of an original by Antonio Canova—apparently a copy of the version that Canova carved for the sixth Duke of Bedford, Woburn Abbey, England. A slightly different and more famous* Three Graces *by Canova is in Leningrad at the Hermitage. The San Simeon copy is signed "Boyer," a name that has never been traced.*

*Right: The lantana growing along the Esplanade were renamed* Lantana montevidensis *'Rotanzi' in 1984 in honor of Norman Rotanzi, a San Simeon employee since 1934 and head groundskeeper for most of that period, who developed the distinctive teardrop shape for these flowering shrubs.*

well-proportioned front panel. Nearby are versions of *The Wrestlers* and *Seated Mercury* by the Romanelli Brothers of Florence, and just around the curve is Fritz Behn's *Europa*.

The tiled walkway to Casa del Sol invites a side trip. A monumental Byzantine fountain hovers over the entry court, and a few feet beyond is a baptismal font of the thirteenth century. Another sarcophagus—or, as some say, a non-funerary basin—stands against the back wall of the court; flanking the nearby entry doors to the building are some intricately detailed Persian tiles.

The Esplanade continues toward Casa del Mar, where *The Three Graces* is situated. Reputed to have been one of Hearst's favorite works, the marble group represents Brilliance, Joy, and Bloom, daughters of the god Zeus. Yet another sarcophagus is displayed alongside, and at each end of this alcove setting stand Roman columns from North Africa, two of the loveliest architectural pieces at San Simeon. Roman, too, are the marble busts that flank the entry to Casa del Mar, which is directly opposite.

From here the Esplanade curves sharply eastward, giving an impressive view of Casa Grande through oaks, magnolias, and palms; a short distance beyond are the Egyptian sculptures mentioned earlier. On the level below and to the right is the South Terrace. Here are found an unusual boat-shaped fountain basin that previously belonged to Pierpont Morgan; and, a short distance away, the old wellhead from Phoebe Hearst's *Hacienda del Pozo de Verona*.

*San Simeon's oldest art works date from the Eighteenth and Nineteenth Egyptian dynasties. Representations of the goddess Sekhmet, the black granite sculptures stare out over the Esplanade and South Terrace toward the Pacific beyond. Julia Morgan designed an Art Deco fountain of dark gray limestone as a setting for the ancient pieces, and she and Hearst chose complimentary Egyptian motifs for the tile risers of the flanking steps.*

*A Spanish armorial wall plaque greeted arriving guests as they climbed the steps below the South Terrace and continued up to the Main Terrace and the front door of Casa Grande.*

*Uncountable thousands of glass tiles from Venice, Italy, are set in mosaic patterns on the sides and floor of the Roman Pool and on the decks, adjoining walls, and massive concrete beams overhead. Here, as at the Neptune Pool, light in all its guises creates the mood. Breathtaking by day, the Roman Pool comes even more into its own at night, when the alabaster and marble lamps glow like little moons in the crystal-clear, silent water.*

***Lower Terraces, Neptune Pool, and Roman Pool.*** Running eastward and southward from the Neptune Pool are the two largest terraces on the grounds. The North Terrace, below Casa del Monte, is decorated with five Renaissance wellheads, the largest and most interesting of which comes from the Palazzo Balbi on the Grand Canal in Venice. The terrace below Casa del Sol, on the other hand, features two modern bronze copies of ancient works, *Victory* and *The Discuss Thrower*. Another bronze statue, a copy of Donatello's *David*, surmounts the nearby two-tiered fountain, which is itself a 1920s copy of the original in the Paseo de la Bomba, Granada.

The Neptune Pool is dominated by an ancient Roman temple, probably of the third or fourth century;

Renaissance sculptures of Neptune and his attendant Nereids—formerly fountain pieces in Italy—occupy its upper section. At poolside and in the alcove across from the temple are *Nymphs and Swans* and the *Birth of Venus,* marble groups carved by Charles Cassou, a French sculptor Hearst commissioned. Matching colonnaded pavilions at the ends of the pool complete what for many visitors is San Simeon's most memorable setting..

Our overview of the estate concludes with the indoor Roman Pool, of which we can truly say, "Last but by no means least." Resplendent with mosaic tile work inspired by the ancient church of Santa Croce in Ravenna, Italy—the so-called mausoleum of Empress Galla Placidia —the Roman Pool is at once stunningly and quietly beautiful.

Reproductions of famous classical sculptures—the work of Carlo Freter of Pietrasanta, Italy—stand at the ends and on one side of the pool; the basin itself is surrounded with sculptured marble lamp standards by the Romanelli Brothers of Florence. And at the back end of the narrow wading alcove stands a seventeenth-century statue of *Abundantia,* whose horn of plenty is often said to symbolize the richness of La Cuesta Encantada.

*Even in the drabbest midday light a sense of magic pervades the Neptune Pool; early morning or late afternoon light intensifies that impression. Yet another mood—no less dramatic or magical—takes hold on occasional fog-enshrouded days.*

*Of all the memorable views at La Cuesta Encantada, perhaps none lingers more enduringly in the mind than that of the Neptune Pool. Julia Morgan's observation about W. R. Hearst and his fabulous dream, recalled years later by one of her associates, comes to mind when one looks out over the water toward the ancient temple portico: "Of course, this is just temporary for his use. The country needs architectural museums, not just places where you hang pictures and sculptures." In creating settings as convincing as this one for the Roman temple, Hearst and Morgan together attained that very ideal.*

TO CARMEL
& MONTEREY

BIG SUR
COUNTRY

MISSION
SAN ANTONIO • JOLON

Jolon Road

Santa Lucia Range

Willow Creek

Cape
San Martin

GORDA

Salmon Creek

Salmon Creek Falls

San Carpoforo Creek

Ragged Point

Rancho
Piedra Blanca

LA CUESTA ENCANTADA
The Enchanted Hill

Lake Nacimiento

Arroyo de la Cruz

POINT PIEDRAS BLANCAS

SAN SIMEON BAY

SAN SIMEON

Rancho San Simeon     San Simeon Creek

San Simeon
State Beach

Site of Stajahuayo
(Indian Rancheria)

CAMBRIA

PACIFIC OCEAN

El Camino Real

Salinas River

Lake San Antonio

101

N
W        E
S

MISSION SAN MI

Almond Trees

PASO ROBLES

Vineyards

TEMPLETON

46

HARMONY

1

POINT ESTERO

CAYUCOS

ATASCADERO

41

Whale Rock
Res.

ESTERO BAY

MORRO BAY

Morro Bay
State Park
& Museum

BAYWOOD PARK

LOS OSOS

41

101

MISSION S
LUIS OBIS

SAN LUIS OBISPO

POINT BUCHON     Montaña de Oro
State Park

HEARST CASTLE
and The
CENTRAL COAST

AVILA BEACH

SAN LUIS OBISPO BAY          SHELL BEACH

PISMO BEACH

GROVER CITY

ARR

OCEANO

0  1  2  3  4  5  6  7  8  9  10
miles

© Oceana Maps 1985